Betty Crocker's Barbecue Cookbook

Photography Director: Remo Cosentino
Illustrations: Ray Skibinski

 **Golden Press/New York**
Western Publishing Company, Inc.
Racine, Wisconsin

First Printing, 1982
Copyright © 1982 by General Mills, Inc., Minneapolis, Minnesota.
All rights reserved. Produced in the U.S.A.
Library of Congress Catalog Card Number: 81-84525
Golden® and Golden Press® are trademarks of Western Publishing Company, Inc.
ISBN 0-307-09933-4

Foreword

Sixty million American families can't be wrong—they love to barbecue. Chances are you're already among this number or anxious to join it. And why not? Barbecuing is one of the most relaxed, convivial kinds of cooking you'll ever encounter. And food cooked on a grill has a flavor and savor that's unique.

Not all that long ago a barbecue was reserved for warm summer days, and the barbecue menu consisted of franks or burgers or steaks. But that's not the way things are anymore! Today a barbecue is meant for year-round enjoyment, and barbecue fare runs the gamut from simple to sumptuous. And this book covers the range, with more than 130 recipes for the grill, the rotisserie and the smoker. We've included traditional favorites, to be sure, but we've also added that special breath of fresh air to a host of other foods. You'll find a wide choice of burgers, some in surprising shapes and with unusual flavors; steaks and chops, just as you like them; chicken, in parts and spit-roasted whole. Included, too, are ribs and roasts, fish and seafood, even a special collection of grill-along vegetables and breads to help make the most of your grill top. Best of all, no special meat cuts are required—you can get everything at the supermarket. You won't want to miss Beer-Basted Bologna Ring or Pork and Pepper Kabobs when you're looking for a change of pace. And although most of the recipes are planned for family-size servings, you'll find a number of selections—Turkey and Vegetable Barbecue and Smoked Salmon, for example—are ideal for larger gatherings. (Speaking of servings, we want you to know that we have planned our servings to provide about one-fourth of the day's protein requirement for an adult. Therefore, even though the servings for some recipes may seem small to you, we assure you they are nutritionally adequate. But if you have a family of hearty eaters, you may want to figure on fewer servings.)

Like so many other things, outdoor cooking does take some getting used to. If you're new to barbecuing, you'll want to review the basics on pages 4 through 6. You'll learn that grills (and instructions for using them) vary from manufacturer to manufacturer. If you're cooking with charcoal, you'll discover that no two fires are ever exactly alike. And then there's the weather, which also affects the outcome. But we've built these variables right into our recipes by offering a range of cooking times and by including additional doneness tests whenever possible. We were able to do this because we tested these recipes just as you'll be using them: We barbecued on calm, hot days as well as on brisk, windy ones, and we used grills of various makes and models. We had great success, and that's why we're sure you will too.

Betty Crocker

Contents

Barbecue Basics

THE GRILLWORKS

The following will give you a good idea of the grills available:

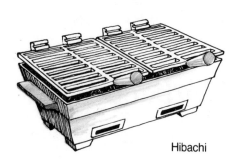

Brazier

Braziers: In its simplest form, a brazier consists of a shallow firebox to hold the charcoal and a metal cooking grill for the food. It may have 3 or 4 legs, long or short, foldable or stationary.

Hibachis: Of Japanese origin, these grills are very portable, permitting you to do on-the-spot cooking almost anywhere. The single hibachi is perfect for cooking small amounts of food; double or triple models are also available.

Hibachi

Covered kettle cookers: Made of heavy cast metal and available in a variety of sizes, these are more sophisticated members of the brazier family. They have air-flow vents, both top and bottom, that help control the heat.

Gas and electric grills: Gas is used to heat semi-permanent lava briquets that act as the cooking "coals" in grills designed like charcoal ones. Gas grills are available as portables (fed by small propane tanks) or as stationaries (connected to your regular gas supply). Electric grills are fast, but they are somewhat limited in mobility because they must be connected to safely grounded outlets or extensions. Always follow the manufacturer's directions carefully when using gas or electric grills.

Smokers: These "slow-cookers" are available in either charcoal or electric models. Ranging from simple to complicated, they promise and deliver food with a unique smoky flavor.

GRILL-HELPERS

Fads, fancies and fashions could make this list almost endless. But do yourself a favor and start with these helpful accessories:

Covered Kettle

- A supply of long-handled utensils (tongs, forks, spatulas and basting brushes) help keep the heat at a distance.
- Fire- and heat-resistant mitts are musts when you have to turn food or arrange the coals with tongs.
- Pump-type water sprayers will help control flare-ups.
- Hinged wire baskets for the grill and spit baskets for the rotisserie make grilling small pieces of food possible and "fall apart" foods (fish, for example) easier to turn.
- Metal skewers, plain or fancy, are essential for kabobs.
- Small grill pans come in handy for heating sauces and bastes.
- An electric charcoal starter makes for fast, odorless beginnings.
- A meat thermometer is the best way to confirm the desired doneness of roasts, steaks and chops. (See also page 24.)

Gas Grill

Smoker

GRILLING WITH CHARCOAL

One important point to remember about grilling with charcoal: Damp charcoal can put a damper on the whole meal by taking forever to start. So always store your charcoal in a *dry* place.

How Much to Use?

Don't overdo. For 4 to 6 servings of a quick-cooking food (hamburgers, for example), use 20 to 30 briquets; 40 to 50 are about right for longer-cooking foods (roasts, pork, poultry, whole fish). You'll need enough briquets to form a solid bed of coals under the grilling area. Any meat or poultry that grills longer than an hour will require about 10 additional briquets per hour. Always place the added briquets around the edges so they touch the already-burning coals.

Getting the Fire Going

Place the desired number of briquets in the firebox and arrange them in a slight pyramid shape to get them ready for lighting. (The pyramid shape allows air to circulate, heating the briquets faster.)

If using an electric starter, pyramid the briquets over the coil and plug in. After the briquets have been started (8 to 12 minutes), remove the starter to an out-of-the-way, fireproof spot. The coals will be ready for grilling in another 15 to 20 minutes.

If using a liquid starter, follow the manufacturer's directions. (Use only liquid starters especially intended for charcoal — never use gasoline or kerosene.) The coals will be ready for grilling in 25 to 45 minutes. Once the fire is under way, never use liquid starter to "speed things up" — the danger of flare-ups and fire is far too great.

No matter how you start the fire, the coals will be ready for grilling when they have a light, even coating of gray ash.

Controlling the Heat

As soon as the coals are ready for grilling, spread them in a single layer in an even pattern just slightly larger than the area covered by the food on the cooking grill.

Try to keep the heat as even as possible throughout the grilling period. To raise the heat, rake the coals closer together and knock off a bit of the ash or lower the cooking grill or open the vents. For a too-hot fire, do just the opposite — spread and separate the coals, raise the cooking grill or partially close the vents.

Occasional flare-ups are part and parcel of grilling. Although they can be controlled easily by covering the grill, a spray of water can be just as effective. Just don't get carried away and soak the coals.

COOKING WITH GAS AND ELECTRICITY

Both gas and electric grills are instant starters, heat up quickly, are easy to control and can continue to supply the desired cooking temperature as long as you want it.

Starting the Gas Grill

Preheat the grill according to the manufacturer's instructions. If the weather is cool or windy, a slightly longer warm-up time as well as a higher setting will speed along the cooking.

Controlling the Heat

You can regulate the heat by adjusting the control, repositioning the cooking grill or covering the grill. The heat varies from brand to brand. A gas grill also has faster and slower cooking areas. Once you map these out, however, you can use them to produce different degrees of doneness.

Grill Care

Unlike charcoal briquets, the lava briquets can be used over and over. But you can avoid flare-ups and lengthen the life of the briquets by turning them over every once in a while, between cooking times, to burn off the grease that accumulates from cooking meat. To avoid corrosion on metal parts of the grill, remove foods from the grill before salting.

COOKING IN A SMOKER

Smoke-cooking takes a lot of time and a lot of charcoal, but if you're a smoked-food fan, it's well worth the investment — the flavor is truly unique. Although each smoker is slightly different, they all work on the same principle. Wet hardwood chips are placed on the hot coals to produce smoke and a pan of water is placed between the heat source and the cooking grill to create moisture. The smoke is maintained by adding wet chips. Always follow the manufacturer's instructions.

Controlling the Heat

Heat is controlled by adjusting the level of the cooking rack and/or regulating the air vents. The more air, the hotter the fire. To maintain a constant heat over the long cooking period, add briquets every hour or as directed in the recipes.

Adding Flavored Smoke

Place hickory, fruitwood or *green* hardwood chips (soaked in water for 30 minutes, then drained) on the burning coals to slow the cooking and create "flavored" smoke. Toss in a few wet chips whenever smoke stops coming out of the vents. Additional flavor can also be provided by brushing cooking sauces on the food before smoking.

BEEF
for the Barbecue

Hamburgers

1 pound ground beef
3 tablespoons water or milk
2 to 3 tablespoons finely chopped
    onion
½ teaspoon salt
¼ teaspoon pepper

Mix all ingredients. Shape mixture into 4 patties, each about 4 inches in diameter.

Grill patties about 4 inches from medium coals, turning once, until desired doneness, 5 to 7 minutes on each side for medium. Serve in split hamburger buns if desired.   4 servings.

Hickory Burgers

1 can (8 ounces) tomato sauce
¼ cup Worcestershire sauce
1 teaspoon sugar
1 teaspoon hickory smoked salt
⅛ teaspoon pepper
1½ pounds ground beef
¼ cup finely chopped onion
6 hamburger buns, split and
    toasted

Heat tomato sauce, Worcestershire sauce, sugar, salt and pepper to boiling over medium heat, stirring constantly; remove from heat. Shape ground beef into 12 patties, each about 4 inches in diameter. Mix ⅓ cup sauce and the onion. Spread each of 6 patties with 1 tablespoon sauce mixture to within ½ inch of edge; top with a remaining patty and seal edge firmly.

Grill patties about 4 inches from medium coals until desired doneness, 5 to 7 minutes for medium; turn patties. Heat remaining sauce in grill pan on grill; brush each patty with sauce. Grill until desired doneness, 5 to 7 minutes for medium. Serve in hamburger buns with any remaining sauce. If desired, insert 6 pimiento-stuffed olives in each of 6 small raw onion rings. Insert wooden pick in onion ring and olive to secure; insert in top of hamburger bun.   6 sandwiches.

Filled Hamburgers

1½ pounds ground beef
¼ cup dry bread crumbs
2 tablespoons water
1 tablespoon Worcestershire sauce
½ teaspoon salt
¼ teaspoon pepper
1 egg
Fillings (right)

Mix all ingredients except Fillings. Shape mixture into 12 patties, each about 4 inches in diameter. Top each of 6 patties with one of the Fillings, spreading to within ½ inch of edge; top with a remaining patty and seal edge firmly.

Grill patties about 4 inches from medium coals, turning once, until desired doneness, 5 to 7 minutes on each side for medium. Serve in split hamburger buns if desired.   6 servings.

Fillings

1 tablespoon finely chopped onion
1 tablespoon chopped tomato
1 tablespoon shredded Cheddar cheese
1 to 2 teaspoons prepared horseradish

Fiesta Burgers

Fiesta Filling (right)
Avocado Topping (right)
1½ pounds ground beef
¼ cup dry bread crumbs
2 tablespoons water
1 tablespoon Worcestershire
   sauce
½ teaspoon salt
¼ teaspoon pepper
1 egg

Prepare Fiesta Filling and Avocado Topping. Mix remaining ingredients. Shape mixture into 12 patties, each about 4 inches in diameter. Spread each of 6 patties with about 2 tablespoons filling to within ½ inch of edge; top with a remaining patty and seal edge firmly.

Grill patties about 4 inches from medium coals, turning once, until desired doneness, 5 to 7 minutes on each side for medium. Serve with Avocado Topping. Serve in hamburger buns if desired.   6 servings.

Fiesta Filling

Mix ¼ cup finely chopped onion, ¼ cup finely chopped tomato and ¼ cup finely chopped green chilies.

Avocado Topping

1 small avocado, cut up
¼ cup dairy sour cream
1 tablespoon lemon juice
⅛ to ¼ teaspoon red pepper sauce

Beat all ingredients with hand beater until smooth.

Stacked Blueburgers

1½ pounds ground beef
1 tablespoon Worcestershire sauce
½ teaspoon garlic salt
¼ teaspoon pepper
1 package (3 ounces) cream
    cheese, softened
2 tablespoons crumbled blue
    cheese
2 teaspoons prepared mustard

Mix ground beef, Worcestershire sauce, garlic salt and pepper. Shape mixture into 12 patties, each about 4 inches in diameter. Mix cream cheese, blue cheese and mustard. Spread each of 6 patties with about 1½ tablespoons cheese mixture to within ½ inch of edge; top with a remaining patty and seal edge firmly.

Grill patties about 4 inches from medium coals, turning once, until desired doneness, 5 to 7 minutes on each side for medium. Serve in sliced kaiser rolls if desired.   6 servings.

Cheeseburgers Italian

1½ pounds ground beef
⅓ cup grated Parmesan cheese
⅓ cup chili sauce
¼ cup finely chopped onion
1 teaspoon dried Italian herb
    seasoning
½ teaspoon salt
¼ teaspoon pepper
1 large tomato, cut into 6 slices
3 slices mozzarella cheese, cut
    into halves, if desired
6 hamburger buns, split and
    toasted

Mix ground beef, Parmesan cheese, chili sauce, onion, herb seasoning, salt and pepper. Shape mixture into 6 patties, each about 4 inches in diameter.

Grill patties about 4 inches from medium coals until desired doneness, 5 to 7 minutes for medium; turn patties. Place tomato slice on each patty. Grill until desired doneness, 5 to 7 minutes for medium, topping each patty with cheese slice during last minute of grilling. Serve in hamburger buns. 6 sandwiches.

Saucy Burgers

1½ pounds ground beef
¼ cup chili sauce
½ teaspoon salt
½ cup chili sauce
2 tablespoons sugar
2 tablespoons finely chopped
    onion
1 tablespoon prepared
    horseradish
1 teaspoon chili powder
½ teaspoon salt
6 kaiser rolls, sliced and toasted

Mix ground beef, ¼ cup chili sauce and ½ teaspoon salt. Shape mixture into 6 patties, each about 5 inches in diameter. Mix remaining ingredients except rolls. Heat to boiling over medium heat, stirring constantly; reduce heat. Simmer uncovered, stirring occasionally, 3 minutes.

Grill patties about 4 inches from medium coals until desired doneness, 3 to 5 minutes for medium; turn patties. Spoon about 2 tablespoons chili sauce mixture on each patty. Grill until desired doneness, 3 to 5 minutes for medium. Serve in rolls.   6 sandwiches.

Bacon Burgers

1½ pounds ground beef
½ cup dry bread crumbs
¼ cup water
¼ cup snipped parsley
1 teaspoon garlic salt
¼ teaspoon pepper
1 egg
6 slices bacon, cut into halves

Mix all ingredients except bacon. Shape mixture into 6 patties, each about 4 inches in diameter. Crisscross 2 half-slices bacon on each patty, tucking ends under and securing with wooden picks.

Grill patties about 4 inches from medium coals, turning once, until desired doneness, 5 to 7 minutes on each side for medium. Serve in split hamburger buns if desired.   6 servings.

Lemon Burgers

1 teaspoon instant beef bouillon
¼ cup hot water
1 pound ground beef
¼ cup dry bread crumbs
1 teaspoon grated lemon peel
¼ teaspoon ground nutmeg
¼ teaspoon salt
¼ teaspoon pepper
1 egg

Dissolve instant bouillon in hot water. Mix bouillon and remaining ingredients. Shape mixture into 4 patties, each about 4 inches in diameter.

Grill patties about 4 inches from medium coals, turning once, until desired doneness, 5 to 7 minutes on each side for medium. Serve in toasted split hamburger buns and garnish with lemon slices if desired.   4 servings.

Deli Burgers

1½ pounds ground beef
¼ cup finely chopped onion
3 tablespoons water
½ teaspoon salt
¼ teaspoon red pepper sauce
1 can (8 ounces) sauerkraut, drained
8 slices Swiss cheese

Mix all ingredients except sauerkraut and cheese. Shape mixture into 8 patties, each about 4 inches in diameter.

Grill patties about 4 inches from medium coals, turning once, until desired doneness, 4 to 6 minutes on each side for medium, topping each with 2 to 3 tablespoons sauerkraut and cheese slice during last minute of grilling. Serve in split rye buns if desired.   8 servings.

Burgundy Burgers

1 pound ground beef
¼ cup dry red wine or cranberry juice
2 tablespoons finely snipped chives
½ teaspoon salt
¼ teaspoon pepper

Mix all ingredients. Shape mixture into 4 patties, each about 4 inches in diameter.

Grill patties about 4 inches from medium coals, turning once, until desired doneness, 5 to 7 minutes on each side for medium. Serve in sliced onion buns if desired.   4 servings.

Mushroom Burgers

1 pound ground beef
2 tablespoons finely chopped onion
2 tablespoons catsup
½ teaspoon salt
⅛ teaspoon pepper
1 jar (2½ ounces) sliced
    mushrooms, drained
4 slices Swiss cheese, if desired

Mix all ingredients except mushrooms and cheese. Shape mixture into 8 patties, each about 4 inches in diameter. Top each of 4 patties with sliced mushrooms to within ½ inch of edges; top with a remaining patty and seal edge firmly.

Grill patties about 4 inches from medium coals, turning once, until desired doneness, 5 to 7 minutes on each side for medium, topping each with cheese slice during last minute of grilling. Serve in split sesame buns if desired.   4 servings.

Smoky Cheeseburgers

1½ pounds ground beef
¼ cup catsup
¼ cup water
1 teaspoon instant minced onion
1 teaspoon Worcestershire sauce
½ teaspoon salt
⅛ teaspoon liquid smoke
6 slices process American cheese

Mix all ingredients except cheese. Shape mixture into 6 patties, each about 4 inches in diameter.

Grill patties about 4 inches from medium coals, turning once, until desired doneness, 5 to 7 minutes on each side for medium, topping each with cheese slice during last minute of grilling. Serve in split rye buns if desired.   6 servings.

Cheeseburgers Deluxe

Mushroom Topping (right)
1½ pounds ground beef
½ cup shredded Cheddar cheese
    (about 2 ounces)
¼ cup dry bread crumbs
¼ cup water
1 teaspoon lemon pepper

Prepare Mushroom Topping; keep warm or reheat after grilling Cheeseburgers. Mix remaining ingredients. Shape mixture into 8 patties, each about 4 inches in diameter.

Grill patties about 4 inches from medium coals, turning once, until desired doneness, 4 to 6 minutes on each side for medium. Serve each with Mushroom Topping. Serve in hamburger buns if desired.   8 servings.

Mushroom Topping
8 ounces small mushrooms, cut
    into halves
¼ cup chopped green onions
    (with tops)
1 tablespoon snipped parsley
2 tablespoons margarine or butter
    Grated Parmesan cheese

Cook and stir all ingredients except cheese in 10-inch skillet until mushrooms are tender, 2 to 3 minutes; sprinkle with cheese.

Beef for the Barbecue   **11**

Sour Cream Burgers

Sour Cream Sauce (right)
1 pound ground beef
3 tablespoons water
½ teaspoon salt
½ teaspoon ground nutmeg
½ teaspoon onion powder
1 medium tomato, cut into
    4 slices

Prepare Sour Cream Sauce; refrigerate. Mix remaining ingredients except tomato slices. Shape mixture into 4 patties, each about 4 inches in diameter.

Grill patties about 4 inches from medium coals, turning once, until desired doneness, 5 to 7 minutes on each side for medium. Top each patty with tomato slice and about 2 tablespoons Sour Cream Sauce. Serve in sliced hard rolls if desired.   4 servings.

Sour Cream Sauce
Mix ½ cup dairy sour cream, ½ teaspoon dried dill weed and ¼ teaspoon salt.

Super Burgers

1½ pounds ground beef
½ cup soft bread crumbs
½ cup chopped green onions
    (with tops)
¼ cup catsup
1 tablespoon prepared
    horseradish
½ teaspoon salt
1 egg
3 slices process American
    cheese, cut diagonally
    into halves
6 small slices dill pickle
3 cherry tomatoes, cut into
    halves

Mix ground beef, bread crumbs, onions, catsup, horseradish, salt and egg. Shape mixture into 6 patties, each about 4 inches in diameter.

Grill patties about 4 inches from medium coals, turning once, until desired doneness, 5 to 7 minutes on each side for medium. Top each patty with cheese slice half. Place pickle slice between 2 tomato halves. Insert wooden pick in tomato to secure; insert in top of patty. Serve open-face on split hamburger buns if desired.   6 servings.

Coney Burgers

1 pound ground beef
1 can (7½ ounces) chili with beans
1 tablespoon chopped green
    chilies
6 frankfurter buns, split and
    warmed

Shape ground beef into 6 rolls, each about 5 inches long and ¾ inch thick. Mix chili with green chilies in small grill pan; heat on grill until hot.

Grill ground beef rolls about 4 inches from medium coals, turning once, until desired doneness, 3 to 5 minutes on each side for medium. Serve in frankfurter buns; spoon about 2 tablespoons chili mixture into each bun.   6 sandwiches.

Tortilla Burgers

1 pound ground beef
½ cup refried beans
¼ cup chopped green chilies
¼ cup chopped onions
1 tablespoon snipped parsley
   Six 7-inch flour tortillas
   Taco sauce

Mix all ingredients except tortillas and taco sauce. Shape mixture into 6 oval patties, each about 4 inches long and 3 inches wide.

Grill patties about 4 inches from medium coals, turning once, until desired doneness, 5 to 7 minutes on each side for medium. Wrap tortillas in aluminum foil. Heat on grill until warm, 4 to 6 minutes. Serve patties in tortillas with taco sauce. Garnish with chopped tomato, snipped parsley and dairy sour cream if desired.   6 servings.

Sandwich Burgers

1 pound ground beef
3 tablespoons water
2 tablespoons dry bread crumbs
1 tablespoon dried parsley flakes
½ teaspoon onion salt
1 egg
8 mild onion rings

Mix all ingredients except onion rings. Shape mixture into 9-inch square on 12-inch waxed paper square with wet fingers. Cut mixture and waxed paper with scissors into 4 squares.

Invert squares on grill; remove waxed paper. Grill about 4 inches from medium coals until desired doneness, 3 to 5 minutes for medium; turn squares. Place 2 onion rings on each square. Grill until desired doneness, 3 to 5 minutes for medium. Serve on buttered toast if desired.   4 servings.

Colossal Burger

1½ pounds ground beef
3 tablespoons water
1 teaspoon salt
½ teaspoon ground sage
¼ cup chopped green onions (with tops)
1 tablespoon prepared horseradish
1 tablespoon prepared mustard
1 package (3 ounces) cream cheese, softened

Mix ground beef, water, salt and sage. Divide mixture into halves. Shape each half into patty, about 8 inches in diameter, on waxed paper. Mix remaining ingredients. Spread mixture over 1 patty to within ½ inch of edge. Invert remaining patty on mixture; remove top sheet of waxed paper. Seal edge firmly. Invert patty on well-greased hinged wire grill basket; remove waxed paper.

Grill patty about 4 inches from medium coals, turning once, until desired doneness, 10 to 12 minutes on each side for medium. Cut into wedges. Garnish with green onions and cherry tomatoes if desired.   6 servings.

Beef Teriyaki on Skewers

1 cup dry red wine
¼ cup packed brown sugar
¼ cup soy sauce
1 tablespoon crushed gingerroot
2 cloves garlic, crushed
2 - pound beef boneless bottom
   or top round steak, cut into
   1-inch cubes
2 teaspoons cornstarch

Mix all ingredients except beef cubes and cornstarch; pour over beef. Cover and refrigerate, turning beef 2 or 3 times, at least 4 hours.

Remove beef; reserve marinade. Thread beef cubes about ¼ inch apart on each of 8 metal skewers. Stir reserved marinade gradually into cornstarch. Cook over medium heat, stirring constantly, until thickened, about 3 minutes.

Cover and grill kabobs 5 to 6 inches from medium coals, turning and brushing 2 or 3 times with marinade mixture, until desired doneness, 15 to 20 minutes for medium.   8 servings.

Microwave Reheat Directions: Remove metal skewers. For 1 serving, place refrigerated beef on microwaveproof plate. Cover loosely and microwave on high (100%) until hot, 1½ to 2 minutes. Let stand 1 minute. For 2 servings, microwave 2½ to 3½ minutes.

Curried Beef and Vegetable Kabobs

¾ cup plain yogurt
¼ cup lemon juice
¼ cup finely chopped onion
1 to 2 teaspoons curry powder
1 teaspoon ground cumin
1 teaspoon salt
¼ teaspoon pepper
1 clove garlic, crushed
1½ - pound beef boneless bottom or
   top round steak, cut into
   1-inch cubes
1 green pepper, cut into 1-inch
   pieces
12 whole mushrooms
12 cherry tomatoes

Mix yogurt, lemon juice, onion, curry, cumin, salt, pepper and garlic; pour over beef cubes. Cover and refrigerate, turning beef 2 or 3 times, at least 4 hours.

Remove beef; reserve marinade. Thread beef cubes about ¼ inch apart on each of 3 metal skewers. Alternate pepper pieces, mushrooms and tomatoes on each of 3 metal skewers, leaving space between foods.

Cover and grill beef kabobs 4 to 5 inches from medium coals, turning and brushing 2 or 3 times with reserved marinade, until desired doneness, 15 to 20 minutes for medium. Cover and grill vegetable kabobs, turning and brushing 2 or 3 times with reserved marinade, until vegetables are crisp-tender, 10 to 20 minutes.   6 servings.

Beef on Skewers

1 cup tomato juice
¼ cup vinegar
2 tablespoons prepared mustard
1 teaspon sugar
1 teaspoon salt
¼ teaspoon pepper
1½-pound beef boneless sirloin
    steak, cut into 1-inch cubes
½ pound mushroom caps
1 large green pepper, cut into
    1-inch pieces
1 pint cherry tomatoes
½ fresh pineapple, cut into pieces

Mix tomato juice, vinegar and seasonings; pour over beef cubes. Cover and refrigerate at least 2 hours.

Remove beef; reserve marinade. Alternate beef cubes, vegetables and pineapple on each of 6 to 8 metal skewers, leaving space between foods.

Cover and grill kabobs 4 to 5 inches from medium coals, turning 2 or 3 times and brushing 4 or 5 times with reserved marinade, until beef is of desired doneness, 20 to 30 minutes for medium.   6 servings.

Charcoal-Broiled Steak

Choose ¾-, 1- or 1½-inch-thick beef steaks. For each serving, allow about ⅓ pound of any beef steak with a bone; allow about ¼ pound for boneless cuts. Slash diagonally outer edge of fat on beef steak at 1-inch intervals to prevent curling (do not cut into lean).

Grill beef 4 to 5 inches from medium coals, turning once or twice, until medium, as directed in Timetable (below).

TIMETABLE

Thickness	Total Grilling Time
¾ inch	10 to 20 minutes
1 inch	18 to 25 minutes
1½ inches	25 to 35 minutes

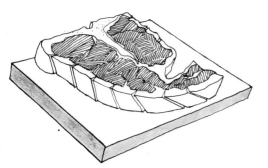

STEAK TIPS

• To prevent the rim of fat around a steak or chop from curling, diagonally slash the outer edge of fat at 1-inch intervals. Be careful not to cut into the lean.

• When testing for doneness, make the cut close to the bone.

• Season each side of the steak only after it has browned nicely. Salt tends to draw moisture to the surface, delaying browning.

Steak au Poivre

1 to 2 tablespoons peppercorns, crushed
2½ - pound beef sirloin steak, 1 to 1½ inches thick
¾ cup water
¼ cup chopped green onions (with tops)
2 tablespoons margarine or butter
1 tablespoon catsup
1 tablespoon steak sauce
1 teaspoon instant beef bouillon
2 tablespoons brandy

Press peppercorns in both sides of beef steak. Grill beef 4 to 5 inches from medium coals, turning 2 or 3 times, until desired doneness, 30 to 35 minutes for medium. Heat remaining ingredients except brandy to boiling, stirring constantly; remove from heat. Stir in brandy. Cut beef into serving pieces. Serve with brandy mixture.   6 to 8 servings.

Microwave Reheat Directions: For 1 serving, place refrigerated beef and sauce on microwaveproof plate. Cover loosely and microwave on medium (50%) until hot, 1½ to 2½ minutes. Let stand 1 minute. For 2 servings, microwave 3 to 4 minutes.

Beer-Barbecued Steak

1 can (7 ounces) beer
¼ cup chili sauce
2 tablespoons vegetable oil
1 tablespoon soy sauce
2 teaspoons Dijon-style mustard
¼ teaspoon red pepper sauce
⅛ teaspoon liquid smoke
1 small onion, coarsely chopped
1 clove garlic, crushed
3 - pound beef sirloin steak, 1 to 1½ inches thick

Mix all ingredients except beef steak. Heat to boiling; reduce heat. Simmer uncovered 30 minutes.

Brush beef with beer mixture. Cover and grill beef 4 to 5 inches from medium coals, turning 2 or 3 times and brushing 4 or 5 times with beer mixture, until desired doneness, 25 to 30 minutes for medium. Cut into serving pieces. Serve with remaining beer mixture.   9 servings.

Seasoned Rib Eye Steaks

⅓ cup lemon juice
2 tablespoons vegetable oil
1 teaspoon seasoned salt
½ teaspoon onion powder
¼ teaspoon garlic powder
¼ teaspoon pepper
4 beef rib eye steaks, ¾ to 1 inch thick

Mix all ingredients except beef steaks; pour over beef. Cover and refrigerate, turning beef 2 or 3 times, at least 1 hour.

Remove beef; reserve marinade. Cover and grill beef 4 to 5 inches from medium coals, turning once and brushing 2 or 3 times with reserved marinade, until desired doneness, 18 to 25 minutes for medium. Cut into serving pieces.   8 servings.

Clockwise from the top: Fiesta Burgers (page 8), Bacon Burgers (page 10), Cheeseburgers Deluxe (page 11) and Super Burgers (page 12).

Pepper and Onion Roast (page 22) and Barbecue Bread (page 68).

Grilled Cube Steaks

4 cloves garlic, finely chopped
¼ cup olive or vegetable oil
1 teaspoon dried rosemary leaves, crushed
½ teaspoon dry mustard
2 teaspoons soy sauce
¼ cup wine vinegar
¼ cup sherry or apple juice
6 beef cubed steaks (about 3 ounces each)

Cook and stir garlic in oil. Add rosemary, mustard and soy sauce; remove from heat. Stir in vinegar and wine; pour over beef steaks. Cover and refrigerate at least 20 minutes.

Remove beef; reserve marinade. Place beef in hinged wire grill basket. Cover and grill beef 4 to 5 inches from medium coals, turning basket 2 or 3 times and brushing beef 2 or 3 times with reserved marinade, until desired doneness, 10 to 15 minutes for medium. Serve in toasted split buns if desired.   6 servings.

Barbecued London Broil

⅓ cup white vinegar
⅓ cup vegetable oil
3 tablespoons packed brown sugar
3 tablespoons soy sauce
2 medium onions, sliced
1 clove garlic, crushed
½ teaspoon coarsely ground pepper
1½-pound beef flank steak

Mix all ingredients except beef flank steak; pour over beef. Cover and refrigerate, turning beef 2 or 3 times, at least 4 hours.

Remove beef and onions; reserve marinade. Cover and grill beef 4 to 5 inches from medium coals, turning and brushing 2 or 3 times with reserved marinade, until desired doneness, 10 to 15 minutes for medium. Cook and stir onions in grill pan on grill until warm. Cut beef diagonally across the grain into very thin slices; top with onions.   6 servings.

Grilled Chuck Steak

2 pounds beef chuck blade steaks, ½ to ¾ inch thick
Unseasoned meat tenderizer
¼ cup finely chopped onion
¼ cup finely chopped green pepper
1 tablespoon vegetable oil
¼ cup catsup
¼ cup dry red wine
1 tablespoon packed brown sugar
½ teaspoon garlic powder
⅛ teaspoon cayenne pepper

Sprinkle beef steaks with meat tenderizer as directed on label. Cook and stir onion and green pepper in oil over medium heat until crisp-tender, 2 to 3 minutes. Stir in remaining ingredients; remove from heat.

Grill beef 4 to 5 inches from medium coals, turning and brushing 2 or 3 times with onion mixture, until desired doneness, 10 to 20 minutes for medium. Top beef with remaining onion mixture; cut beef into thin slices.   8 servings.

Ranch Steak

½ cup finely chopped onion
½ cup dry red wine
2 tablespoons vegetable oil
1 teaspoon dry mustard
1 teaspoon salt
¼ teaspoon red pepper sauce
1 clove garlic, crushed
1½-pound beef boneless bottom or
    top round steak, about 1 inch
    thick
½ cup chili sauce

Mix all ingredients except beef steak and chili sauce; pour over beef. Cover and refrigerate, turning beef 2 or 3 times, at least 4 hours.

Remove beef; stir chili sauce into marinade. Cover and grill beef 4 to 5 inches from medium coals, turning and brushing 2 or 3 times with marinade mixture, until desired doneness, 20 to 30 minutes for medium. Cut beef into ½-inch-thick slices. Heat remaining marinade mixture in grill pan on grill. Serve with beef.   6 servings.

Microwave Reheat Directions: For 1 serving, place refrigerated beef and sauce on microwaveproof plate. Cover loosely and microwave on medium (50%) until hot, 1½ to 2½ minutes. Let stand 1 minute. For 2 servings, microwave 3 to 4 minutes.

Liver Venetian

½ cup dry red wine
¼ cup chopped green onions
    (with tops)
2 tablespoons vegetable oil
1 tablespoon lemon juice
½ teaspoon dried sage leaves,
    crushed
½ teaspoon dried basil leaves
¼ teaspoon pepper
1½-pound beef liver, about
    1½ inches thick

Mix all ingredients except beef liver; pour over liver. Cover and refrigerate, turning liver once, at least 1 hour.

Remove liver; reserve marinade. Cover and grill liver 4 to 5 inches from medium coals, turning and brushing 2 or 3 times with reserved marinade, until desired doneness, 15 to 20 minutes for medium (160°). Spoon remaining chopped green onions from marinade over liver. Cut liver into thin slices. 8 servings.

Tomato-Glazed Short Ribs

4 pounds beef short ribs, cut into
    serving pieces
    Unseasoned meat tenderizer
1 can (8 ounces) tomato sauce
¼ cup red wine
1 teaspoon onion powder
⅛ teaspoon red pepper sauce
2 cloves garlic, crushed

Sprinkle beef ribs with meat tenderizer as directed on label. Mix remaining ingredients; pour over beef. Cover and refrigerate, turning beef 2 or 3 times, at least 4 hours.

Remove beef; reserve marinade. Cover and grill beef 4 to 5 inches from medium coals, turning and brushing 4 or 5 times with reserved marinade, until desired doneness, 35 to 45 minutes for medium.   8 to 10 servings.

Microwave Reheat Directions: For 1 serving, place refrigerated beef on microwaveproof plate. Cover loosely and microwave on high (100%) until hot, 2 to 3 minutes. Let stand 1 minute. For 2 servings, microwave 3 to 5 minutes.

Tangy Short Ribs

Zippy Horseradish Sauce (right)
4 *pounds beef short ribs, cut into serving pieces*
½ *cup lemon juice*
½ *cup vegetable oil*
1 *clove garlic, crushed*
1 *teaspoon salt*
1 *teaspoon ground cumin*
¼ *teaspoon pepper*
⅓ *cup steak sauce*

Prepare Zippy Horseradish Sauce. Place beef ribs in shallow glass or plastic dish. Mix remaining ingredients except steak sauce; pour over beef. Cover and refrigerate, turning beef 2 or 3 times, at least 24 hours.

Place beef in spit basket; fasten securely. Cover and cook beef on rotisserie about 4 inches from low heat until well done, about 2 hours; brush beef 2 or 3 times with steak sauce during last 15 minutes of cooking. Serve with Zippy Horseradish Sauce.   8 to 10 servings.

Zippy Horseradish Sauce
¼ *cup mayonnaise or salad dressing*
¼ *cup dairy sour cream*
2 *tablespoons horseradish, well drained*
2 *tablespoons snipped parsley*
½ *teaspoon salt*

Mix all ingredients; cover and refrigerate at least 1 hour.

Marinated Beef Shanks

½ *cup vinegar*
1 *tablespoon dried parsley flakes*
2 *tablespoons steak sauce*
1 *tablespoon vegetable oil*
½ *teaspoon dried basil leaves*
½ *teaspoon salt*
1 *clove garlic, crushed*
4 *beef center cut shank slices, about 1 inch thick (about 2 pounds)*
Unseasoned meat tenderizer

Mix all ingredients except beef shank slices and meat tenderizer; pour over beef. Cover and refrigerate, turning beef 2 or 3 times, at least 4 hours.

Remove beef; reserve marinade. Sprinkle beef with meat tenderizer as directed on label. Cover and grill beef 5 to 6 inches from medium coals, turning and brushing 2 or 3 times with reserved marinade, until desired doneness, 30 to 35 minutes for medium.   4 servings.

Microwave Reheat Directions: For 1 serving, place refrigerated beef on microwaveproof plate. Cover loosely and microwave on medium (50%) until hot, 1½ to 2½ minutes. Let stand 1 minute. For 2 servings, microwave 3 to 4 minutes.

Marinated Rump Roast

1 cup orange juice
1 cup tomato juice
¼ cup vegetable oil
1 clove garlic, crushed
2 teaspoons salt
½ teaspoon ground allspice
¼ teaspoon chili powder
3- to 4-pound beef rolled rump
      roast
3 tablespoons flour
⅓ cup water

Mix juices, oil, garlic, salt, allspice and chili powder; pour over beef roast. Cover and refrigerate, turning beef 2 or 3 times, at least 4 hours.

Remove beef; reserve 2 cups marinade. Insert spit rod lengthwise through center of beef; hold firmly in place with adjustable holding forks. Cook beef on rotisserie about 4 inches from low heat until desired doneness, 1 to 1½ hours for medium (160°).

Mix flour and water; stir into reserved marinade. Heat to boiling, stirring constantly. Boil and stir 1 minute. Cut beef into thin slices; serve marinade mixture over beef.   12 to 16 servings.

Pepper and Onion Roast

3- pound beef cross rib pot roast,
      about 1½ inches thick
1 envelope (.8 ounce) meat
      marinade
2 large red or green peppers, cut
      into ¼-inch strips
1 large white or red onion, cut into
      halves and thinly sliced
¼ cup olive or vegetable oil
1 clove garlic, crushed
1 tablespoon vinegar
1 teaspoon dried oregano leaves
½ teaspoon salt
¼ teaspoon pepper

Marinate beef roast as directed on envelope. Cook and stir red peppers and onion in oil in 10-inch skillet over medium heat until crisp-tender, 3 to 5 minutes. Stir in remaining ingredients; remove from heat.

Cover and grill beef 4 to 5 inches from medium coals, turning 2 or 3 times, until desired doneness, 40 to 50 minutes for medium. Heat and stir pepper and onion mixture on grill until warm. Top beef with pepper and onion mixture; cut beef into thin slices.   9 servings.

Barbecued Chuck Roast

2 cloves garlic, crushed
¼ cup olive or vegetable oil
¼ cup wine vinegar
¼ cup sherry or apple juice
2 teaspoons soy sauce
1 teaspoon dried rosemary leaves,
      crushed
½ teaspoon dry mustard
3- to 4-pound beef chuck roast,
      2½ to 3 inches thick
2 tablespoons catsup

Mix all ingredients except beef roast and catsup; pour over beef. Cover and refrigerate, turning beef 4 or 5 times, at least 24 hours.

Remove beef; stir catsup into marinade. Cover and grill beef 4 to 5 inches from medium coals, turning and brushing 4 or 5 times with marinade mixture, until desired doneness, 1 to 1¼ hours for medium. Cut into serving pieces.   9 servings.

Rotisserie Beef Roast

Insert spit rod lengthwise through center of 5-pound beef boneless rolled rib roast; hold firmly in place with adjustable holding forks. Place foil drip pan under roasting area.

Cover and cook beef on rotisserie about 4 inches from low heat as directed in Timetable (below); brush beef 2 or 3 times with Peppy Tomato Barbecue Sauce or Wine Barbecue Sauce (below) during last 15 minutes of cooking. Remove beef from rotisserie when meat thermometer registers 5 to 10° lower than desired doneness. Remove spit rod; let beef stand in warm place 15 minutes before carving.   14 or 15 servings.

Peppy Tomato Barbecue Sauce

½ cup chili sauce
1 tablespoon vinegar
1 tablespoon molasses
1 teaspoon garlic salt
¼ teaspoon red pepper sauce

Mix all ingredients.

Wine Barbecue Sauce

⅓ cup dry red wine
⅓ cup chili sauce
1 tablespoon vegetable oil
1 clove garlic, crushed
¼ teaspoon red pepper sauce

Mix all ingredients.

TIMETABLE

Internal Temperature	Minutes per Pound
Rare (140°)	20 to 25
Medium (160°)	30 to 35
Well (170°)	40

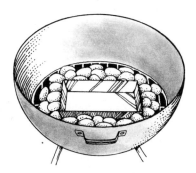

ROASTING TIPS

For best results, rotisserie cooking requires an even ring of coals around the drip pan under the grilling area. It's important to maintain even heat, so be sure to add coals every hour. Brush the roast with sauce *only* during the last 15 minutes of cooking — otherwise, the sauce will burn.

Rotisserie Sirloin

1½ cups chopped mushrooms
2 medium stalks celery, chopped
   (about 1 cup)
1 large onion, finely chopped
¼ cup snipped parsley
2 cloves garlic, crushed
1 teaspoon dried marjoram
   leaves
1 teaspoon salt
2 tablespoons vegetable oil
4 - pound beef boneless tip roast

Cook and stir all ingredients except beef roast over medium heat until celery is crisp-tender, 3 to 5 minutes; remove from heat. Cut beef roast lengthwise down center to within ½ inch of opposite side (additional cuts may be necessary depending on shape of roast). Spread beef open; spread with vegetable mixture to within 1 inch of edges. Roll up beef; tie 3 or 4 times crosswise and twice lengthwise with heavy string. Insert spit rod lengthwise through center of beef; hold firmly in place with adjustable holding forks.

Cook beef on rotisserie about 4 inches from low heat until desired doneness, 1¾ to 2¼ hours for medium (160°). Remove spit rod; let beef stand in warm place 15 minutes before carving.   14 or 15 servings.

Microwave Reheat Directions: For 1 serving, place refrigerated sliced beef on microwaveproof plate. Cover loosely and microwave on medium (50%) until hot, 1 to 2 minutes. Let stand 1 minute. For 2 servings, microwave 2 to 3 minutes.

Rotisserie Beef Brisket

3 - pound well-trimmed fresh beef
   boneless brisket, rolled and
   tied
¼ cup catsup
2 tablespoons soy sauce
1 tablespoon vegetable oil
2 cloves garlic, crushed

Insert spit rod lengthwise through center of beef; hold firmly in place with adjustable holding forks. Mix remaining ingredients.

Cook beef on rotisserie about 4 inches from low heat until desired doneness, 70 to 90 minutes for medium (160°); brush beef 2 or 3 times with catsup mixture during last 15 minutes of cooking. Remove spit rod; let beef stand in warm place 15 minutes before carving.   12 servings.

RARE, MEDIUM OR WELL?

Your roast may look done on the outside, but only a meat thermometer will indicate the degree of doneness inside. A special barbecue meat thermometer will withstand the high temperature of the grill and can be used during the entire cooking time. A regular meat thermometer will not take the intense heat for long and should be used only for testing, toward the end of the cooking period. There's also an instant-reading meat thermometer for immediate answers.

PORK, LAMB and VEAL
for the Barbecue

Frankfurter Specials

Prepare frankfurters using any of the following variations. Grill frankfurters 5 to 6 inches from medium coals, turning 4 or 5 times, until heated through, 12 to 15 minutes.

Franks 'n Onions: For each serving, fry 1 slice bacon 2 minutes on each side. Cut frankfurter lengthwise almost through to bottom; place 1 green onion in cut. Wrap frankfurter with bacon; secure with wooden picks.

Glazed Franks: For each serving, make diagonal cuts in frankfurter almost through to bottom. Mix 1 tablespoon packed brown sugar and 1½ teaspoons horseradish; brush on frankfurter.

Meloned Franks: For each serving, fry 1 slice bacon 2 minutes on each side. Cut frankfurter lengthwise almost through to bottom; place 1 cantaloupe spear in cut. Wrap frankfurter with bacon; secure with wooden picks.

Oriental Franks: For each serving, fry 1 slice bacon 2 minutes on each side. Cut frankfurter lengthwise almost through to bottom; place 3 mandarin orange segments in cut. Wrap frankfurter with bacon; secure with wooden picks.

Tahitian Franks: For each serving, fry 1 slice bacon 2 minutes on each side. Cut frankfurter lengthwise almost through to bottom; place 1 pineapple spear in cut. Wrap frankfurter with bacon; secure with wooden picks.

Plum-Good Franks

½ cup (5 ounces) plum preserves
1 tablespoon lemon juice
¼ teaspoon ground ginger
1 pound frankfurters
8 to 10 frankfurter buns, split and buttered

Heat preserves, lemon juice and ginger to boiling, stirring constantly; reduce heat. Simmer uncovered, stirring constantly, 5 minutes. Make diagonal cuts ¼ inch deep in each frankfurter.

Grill frankfurters 5 to 6 inches from medium coals, turning and brushing 4 or 5 times with preserve mixture, until frankfurters are heated through, 10 to 15 minutes. Grill buns, buttered sides down, until toasted, 3 to 4 minutes. Serve frankfurters in buns.   8 to 10 servings.

Paul Bunyan Frank

3 cups hickory wood chips
1 cup catsup
½ cup vinegar
½ cup molasses
⅓ cup prepared mustard
2 tablespoons Worcestershire sauce
¼ to ½ teaspoon red pepper sauce
3½- to 4-pound piece large bologna

Cover hickory chips with water. Let stand 30 minutes; drain. Mix remaining ingredients except bologna; reserve. Arrange hot coals around edge of firebox; place foil drip pan under grilling area. Remove casing from bologna. Add half of the hickory chips to hot coals.

Cover and grill bologna over drip pan and 5 to 6 inches from medium coals, turning 2 or 3 times and brushing 4 or 5 times with reserved catsup mixture, until bologna is done, 1 to 1¼ hours. Add soaked hickory chips every 30 minutes. Cut bologna into slices. Serve with any remaining catsup mixture and, if desired, in individual French rolls.   10 servings.

Beer-Basted Bologna Ring

1 ring (1 pound) bologna
½ cup beer
1 teaspoon dry mustard
1 teaspoon onion powder

Make 6 diagonal cuts ¼ inch deep in bologna. Mix remaining ingredients; pour over bologna. Cover and refrigerate at least 30 minutes.

Remove bologna; reserve marinade. Cover and grill bologna 5 to 6 inches from medium coals, turning and brushing 2 or 3 times with reserved marinade, until bologna is brown and done, 12 to 15 minutes. Cut into serving pieces. Serve with Grilled German Potato Salad (page 67) if desired.   3 servings.

Pork and Pepper Kabobs

2 pounds pork boneless shoulder,
    cut into 1½-inch cubes
1 can (15 ounces) tomato sauce
1 envelope (1.25 ounces) taco
    seasoning mix
1 tablespoon vegetable oil
1 jar (22 ounces) red and green
    cherry peppers, drained
4 medium zucchini, cut into
    1½-inch pieces

Place pork cubes in saucepan; add enough water to cover. Heat to boiling; reduce heat. Cover and simmer until tender, 25 to 30 minutes; drain.

Mix tomato sauce, taco seasoning mix and oil. Pour over pork; stir to coat. Cover and refrigerate at least 1 hour.

Remove pork; reserve marinade. Alternate pork cubes, peppers and zucchini pieces on each of 6 metal skewers, leaving space between foods. Cover and grill kabobs 5 to 6 inches from medium coals, turning and brushing 2 or 3 times with reserved marinade, until pork is done and no longer pink in center (170°), 20 to 30 minutes.   6 servings.

Pressure Cooker Directions: Place pork cubes and 1 cup water in 4-quart pressure cooker. Following manufacturer's instructions, cover and cook at 15 pounds pressure 12 minutes; reduce pressure and drain. Continue as directed.

Italian Sausage Kabobs

½ cup pizza sauce
1 tablespoon dried basil leaves
1 tablespoon vegetable oil
1½ pounds Italian-style sausages,
    cut into 1½-inch pieces
2 medium zucchini, cut into
    1-inch pieces
1 medium red pepper, cut into
    1½-inch pieces
1 medium green pepper, cut into
    1½-inch pieces
6 large pimiento-stuffed olives

Mix pizza sauce, basil and oil; reserve. Cook sausage pieces in 10-inch skillet over medium heat until partially cooked, about 10 minutes; drain. Alternate sausage pieces, zucchini pieces and red and green pepper pieces on each of 6 metal skewers, leaving space between foods. Place olive on tip of each skewer.

Cover and grill kabobs 5 to 6 inches from medium coals, turning and brushing 2 or 3 times with reserved pizza sauce mixture, until sausage is done and vegetables are crisp-tender, 20 to 25 minutes.   6 servings.

KABOB TIPS

- Kabobs require a solid bed of coals slightly larger than the area needed for the food on the skewers.
- Use separate skewers for meats and vegetables with different grilling times. Partially cook onions and other slow-cooking vegetables before adding to skewers.
- Leave a little space between the food you thread on the skewer — tightly packed food will not cook evenly.

Curried Pork Cutlets

2 limes
1 to 2 teaspoons curry powder
1/2 teaspoon onion powder
1/2 teaspoon salt
4 pork cubed steaks (about 1 pound)

Cut 1/2 lime into 4 slices; reserve. Squeeze juice from remaining 1 1/2 limes; mix with curry powder, onion powder and salt. Pour over pork steaks; turn pork 2 or 3 times.

Remove pork; reserve marinade. Cover and grill pork 5 to 6 inches from medium coals, turning and brushing 2 or 3 times with reserved marinade, until pork is done and no longer pink in center (170°), 15 to 20 minutes. Garnish with reserved lime slices.   4 servings.

Marinated Pork Chops

3 tablespoons packed brown sugar
3 tablespoons bourbon
3 tablespoons soy sauce
1/4 teaspoon ground ginger
4 pork loin or rib chops, 3/4 inch thick

Mix all ingredients except pork chops; pour over pork. Cover and refrigerate, turning pork 2 or 3 times, at least 4 hours.

Remove pork; reserve marinade. Cover and grill pork 5 to 6 inches from medium coals, turning 3 or 4 times and brushing 2 or 3 times with reserved marinade, until pork is done and no longer pink in center (170°), 20 to 30 minutes. Serve with hot buttered noodles sprinkled with grated Parmesan cheese if desired.   4 servings.

Goober Pork Chops

1 cup croutons
1/2 cup finely chopped salted peanuts
2 tablespoons instant minced onion
2 tablespoons finely snipped parsley
1/2 to 1 teaspoon crushed red chili pepper
1/3 cup margarine or butter, melted
1 tablespoon water
3/4 teaspoon salt
8 pork rib chops, about 1 inch thick (with pockets cut into chops on bone side)
1/2 cup apple jelly
1 tablespoon lemon juice

Mix croutons, peanuts, onion, parsley and chili pepper in bowl. Mix margarine, water and salt. Pour over crouton mixture; toss. Stuff pork chop pockets with crouton mixture; secure with wooden picks. Heat jelly and lemon juice just to boiling, stirring constantly.

Cover and grill pork 5 to 6 inches from medium coals until done and no longer pink in center (170°), 50 to 60 minutes; turn pork 3 or 4 times and brush with jelly mixture 2 or 3 times during last 30 minutes of grilling. Remove wooden picks.   8 servings.

Smoked Pork Chops

1 cup apple cider
¼ cup chopped green onions (with tops)
2 tablespoons lemon juice
5 small smoked pork loin or rib chops, ½ inch thick
2 teaspoons cornstarch
1 can (20 ounces) sliced apples, drained

Mix apple cider, green onions and lemon juice; pour over pork chops. Cover and refrigerate, turning pork 2 or 3 times, at least 1 hour.

Remove pork; reserve marinade. Cover and grill pork 5 to 6 inches from medium coals, turning 3 or 4 times, until pork is done and no longer pink in center (170°), 15 to 20 minutes. Stir ¼ cup reserved marinade into cornstarch; mix in remaining marinade. Cook over medium heat, stirring constantly, until mixture thickens and boils. Boil and stir 1 minute. Stir in apple slices; heat through. Serve with pork.   5 servings.

Texas Pork Steaks

1 teaspoon chili powder
½ teaspoon garlic powder
½ teaspoon dry mustard
½ teaspoon salt
¼ teaspoon pepper
2 pounds pork blade or arm steaks, ½ inch thick

Mix all ingredients except pork steaks; rub on pork. Cover and grill pork 5 to 6 inches from medium coals, turning 3 or 4 times, until pork is done and no longer pink in center (170°), 25 to 35 minutes.   6 servings.

Microwave Reheat Directions: For 1 serving, place refrigerated pork on microwaveproof plate. Cover loosely and microwave on medium (50%) until hot, 1½ to 2½ minutes. Let stand 1 minute. For 2 servings, microwave 3 to 4 minutes.

Pork Steaks Oriental

3 tablespoons orange-flavored liqueur
3 tablespoons soy sauce
½ teaspoon ground nutmeg
1 clove garlic, crushed
2 pounds pork arm or blade steaks, ½ inch thick

Mix all ingredients except pork steaks; pour over pork. Cover and refrigerate, turning pork 2 or 3 times, at least 4 hours.

Remove pork; reserve marinade. Cover and grill pork 5 to 6 inches from medium coals, turning 3 or 4 times and brushing 2 or 3 times with reserved marinade, until pork is done and no longer pink in center (170°), 20 to 30 minutes. Garnish with mandarin orange segments and watercress if desired. 6 servings.

Gingered Ham Slice

¼ cup corn syrup
¼ cup ginger ale
1 tablespoon crushed fresh
   gingerroot or ¼ teaspoon
   ground ginger
1 can (15½ ounces) sliced
   pineapple, drained
1 fully cooked smoked ham slice,
   1 inch thick (about 2 pounds)

Mix corn syrup, ginger ale and gingerroot; reserve. Place pineapple in greased hinged wire grill basket.

Cover and grill ham 5 to 6 inches from medium coals, turning and brushing 2 or 3 times with reserved ginger mixture, until ham is done (140°), 20 to 25 minutes. Cover and grill pineapple, turning basket once and brushing pineapple 2 or 3 times with ginger mixture, until heated through, about 10 minutes. Brush ham with ginger mixture. Cut into serving pieces. Garnish with pineapple slices. Sprinkle with snipped parsley if desired.   6 servings.

Maple Ham Slice

¼ cup maple syrup
1 teaspoon dry mustard
½ teaspoon ground allspice
1 fully cooked smoked ham slice,
   1 inch thick (about 2 pounds)
   Whole cloves

Mix maple syrup, mustard and allspice; reserve. Slash ham at 1-inch intervals; insert cloves. Cover and grill ham 5 to 6 inches from medium coals, turning and brushing 2 or 3 times with syrup mixture, until ham is done (140°), 20 to 25 minutes. Remove cloves from ham; brush ham with syrup mixture. Cut into serving pieces. Garnish with spiced peaches and celery leaves if desired.   6 servings.

Ham Hawaiian

1 fully cooked smoked center-cut
   ham slice, 1½ inches thick
   (about 3 pounds)
1 can (9 ounces) cream of coconut
1 can (11 ounces) mandarin
   orange segments, drained
   (reserve syrup)
¼ teaspoon ground allspice
1 tablespoon cornstarch
½ cup raisins
¼ cup flaked coconut
1 tablespoon vinegar

Slash diagonally outer edge of fat of ham slice. Mix ⅓ cup cream of coconut, 2 teaspoons reserved mandarin orange syrup and the allspice. Cover and grill ham 5 to 6 inches from medium coals, turning 2 or 3 times and brushing 4 or 5 times with cream of coconut mixture, until ham is done (140°), 30 to 40 minutes.

Add enough cold water to remaining mandarin orange syrup to measure 1 cup; stir in cornstarch and remaining cream of coconut. Cook over medium heat, stirring constantly, until mixture thickens and boils. Boil and stir 1 minute. Stir in mandarin orange segments, raisins, coconut and vinegar. Cut ham into serving pieces; serve hot orange segment mixture over ham. 9 servings.

Smoked Chutney Spareribs

3 cups hickory wood chips
1 bottle (12½ ounces) chutney
2 tablespoons lemon juice
2 tablespoons Worcestershire
    sauce
½ teaspoon salt
¼ teaspoon red pepper sauce
3 - pound rack fresh pork spareribs,
    cut into halves

Cover hickory chips with water. Let stand 30 minutes; drain. Mix remaining ingredients except pork spareribs; pour over spareribs. Cover and refrigerate, turning spareribs once, at least 1 hour.

Remove spareribs; reserve marinade. Add 1 cup hickory chips to hot charcoal. Fill water pan with water. Place spareribs, bone sides down, on rack about 6 inches from water pan over coals.

Cover smoker and smoke-cook spareribs, brushing with reserved marinade every hour, until spareribs are done and meat begins to pull away from bones (170°), 3 to 4 hours. Add charcoal and soaked hickory chips every hour (add water to pan during cooking if necessary). Cut spareribs into serving pieces. Serve with any remaining marinade if desired.
5 servings.

Smokehouse Spareribs

3 cups hickory wood chips
½ cup vinegar
½ cup Worcestershire sauce
½ cup margarine or butter, melted
½ teaspoon salt
¼ teaspoon red pepper sauce
2 racks fresh pork spareribs
    (about 6 pounds)

Cover hickory chips with water. Let stand 30 minutes; drain. Mix remaining ingredients except pork spareribs; brush on spareribs. Arrange hot coals around edge of firebox; place foil drip pan under grilling area. Add half of the hickory chips to hot coals.

Cover and grill spareribs, bone sides down, over drip pan and 5 to 6 inches from medium coals until done and meat begins to pull away from bone (170°), 1¾ to 2¼ hours; turn and brush spareribs every 10 minutes with vinegar mixture during last 40 minutes of grilling. Add soaked hickory chips and coals every 30 minutes to maintain smoke and even heat. Cut spareribs into serving pieces.   10 servings.

KNOW YOUR RIBS

Country-style spareribs are the meatiest, having the largest ratio of meat to bone. Loin back ribs have a thick layer of meat and are therefore a good choice for smoking or rotisserie cooking. Spareribs have a thin layer of meat on rib bones. Whatever type of ribs you use, figure on ¾ pound per serving.

Barbecued Country Spareribs

1 teaspoon garlic powder
1 teaspoon onion powder
1 teaspoon salt
4½ pounds fresh pork country-
style spareribs, cut into
serving pieces
⅔ cup catsup
2 tablespoons Worcestershire
sauce
1 tablespoon dry mustard
1 teaspoon chili powder
½ teaspoon liquid smoke
¼ teaspoon red pepper sauce

Mix garlic powder, onion powder and salt; rub on pork spare-ribs. Place spareribs, bone sides down, on rack in shallow roasting pan. Roast uncovered in 325° oven 1 hour.

Mix remaining ingredients; reserve. Cover and grill spareribs 5 to 6 inches from medium coals, turning and brushing 2 or 3 times with reserved catsup mixture, until spareribs are done and meat begins to pull away from bones (170°), 20 to 30 minutes. Pour remaining catsup mixture over spareribs before serving.   8 servings.

Pressure Cooker Directions: Place spareribs, 1½ cups water, the garlic powder, onion powder and salt in 6-quart pressure cooker. Following manufacturer's instructions, cover and cook at 15 pounds pressure 15 minutes; reduce pressure and drain. Continue as directed.

Microwave Reheat Directions: For 1 serving, place refrigerated spareribs on microwaveproof plate. Cover loosely and microwave on high (100%) until hot, 2 to 3 minutes. Let stand 1 minute. For 2 servings, microwave 3 to 5 minutes.

Spit-Barbecued Ribs

1 cup soy sauce
½ cup dry white wine or pineapple
juice
2 tablespoons honey
1 clove garlic, crushed
3- to 4-pound rack fresh pork loin
back ribs
¼ cup honey

Mix all ingredients except pork back ribs and ¼ cup honey; pour over ribs. Cover and refrigerate, turning ribs 2 or 3 times, at least 4 hours.

Remove ribs. Lace ribs on spit rod; hold firmly in place with adjustable holding forks. Cover and cook ribs on rotisserie about 4 inches from low heat until done and meat begins to pull away from bone (170°), 1¼ to 1¾ hours; brush ribs 2 or 3 times with ¼ cup honey during last 15 minutes of cooking. Cut into serving pieces.   5 servings.

Barbecued Ribs

4½-pound rack fresh pork loin
    back ribs
3 cups water
½ cup soy sauce
1 tablespoon plus 1½ teaspoons
    cornstarch
Sweet and Sour Sauce (right)

Place pork back ribs in Dutch oven; add water. Heat to boiling; reduce heat. Cover and simmer 5 minutes. Remove ribs; drain on paper towels. Mix soy sauce and cornstarch; brush on ribs. Continue brushing both sides of ribs with soy sauce mixture every 10 minutes, allowing mixture to penetrate pork, until mixture is gone.

Cover and grill ribs 5 to 6 inches from medium coals, brushing with Sweet and Sour Sauce every 3 minutes, until ribs are done and meat begins to pull away from bone (170°), 15 to 20 minutes. Cut into serving pieces. Serve with remaining sauce. 8 servings.

Sweet and Sour Sauce

1 cup water
1 cup catsup
¼ cup packed brown sugar
¼ cup vinegar
¼ cup Worcestershire sauce
1 tablespoon celery seed
1 teaspoon chili powder
1 teaspoon salt
    Few drops red pepper sauce
    Dash of pepper

Heat all ingredients to boiling; remove from heat.

Pork Roast Jubilee

1 can (21 ounces) cherry pie filling
¼ cup brandy
1 tablespoon lemon juice
½ teaspoon ground nutmeg
3-pound fresh pork boneless top
    loin roast, rolled and tied

Mix all ingredients except pork roast; reserve. Insert spit rod lengthwise through center of pork; hold firmly in place with adjustable holding forks.

Cover and cook pork on rotisserie about 4 inches from low heat until done and no longer pink in center (170°), 2 to 2½ hours; brush pork 2 or 3 times with juice of reserved cherry mixture during last 15 minutes of cooking. Heat remaining cherry mixture until hot. Cut pork into serving pieces. Serve cherry mixture with pork.   8 servings.

Cranberry-Glazed Rotisserie Pork Roast

3 - pound fresh pork boneless blade
    Boston roast, rolled and tied
2 teaspoons salt
½ cup frozen cranberry juice
    concentrate, thawed
2 tablespoons packed brown
    sugar
1 teaspoon dry mustard

Place pork roast in Dutch oven. Add just enough water to cover; add salt. Heat to boiling; reduce heat. Cover and simmer 1 hour.

Mix remaining ingredients; reserve. Insert spit rod lengthwise through center of pork; hold firmly in place with adjustable holding forks. Cover and cook pork on rotisserie about 4 inches from low heat until done and no longer pink in center (170°), 1¼ to 2 hours; brush 2 or 3 times with cranberry juice mixture during last 15 minutes of cooking. Cut into serving pieces; serve with remaining cranberry juice mixture.   9 servings.

Pressure Cooker Directions: Place pork roast, 2 cups water and the salt in 4-quart pressure cooker. Following manufacturer's instructions, cover and cook at 15 pounds pressure 30 minutes; reduce pressure and drain. Continue as directed.

Microwave Reheat Directions: For 1 serving, place sliced refrigerated pork on microwaveproof plate. Cover loosely and microwave on medium (50%) until hot, 1½ to 2½ minutes. Let stand 1 minute. For 2 servings, microwave 3 to 4 minutes.

Roast Pork and Orange Sauce

1 can (12 ounces) frozen orange
    juice concentrate, thawed
2 cups water
½ cup packed brown sugar
2 teaspoons salt
1 teaspoon crushed dried
    marjoram leaves
1 teaspoon crushed dried
    rosemary leaves
½ teaspoon coarsely ground
    pepper
6 - pound fresh pork sirloin roast,
    hipbone removed and
    backbone loosened
¼ cup water
1 tablespoon cornstarch

Mix all ingredients except pork roast, ¼ cup water and the cornstarch; pour over pork. Cover and refrigerate, turning pork occasionally, at least 8 hours.

Remove pork; reserve marinade. Tie pork with heavy string. Insert spit rod lengthwise through center of pork; hold firmly in place with adjustable holding forks. Cover and cook pork on rotisserie about 4 inches from low heat until done and no longer pink in center (170°), 2½ to 3 hours; brush pork 2 or 3 times with reserved marinade during last 30 minutes of cooking.

Stir ¼ cup water into cornstarch; stir in remaining marinade. Cook over medium heat, stirring constantly, until mixture thickens and boils. Boil and stir 1 minute. Cut pork into serving pieces; serve marinade mixture with pork. Garnish with orange slices, spiced crabapple and parsley if desired.   16 servings.

Roast Pork and Orange Sauce (page 34).

Alternate food on metal skewers, leaving space between foods for more even cooking.

For grills without a cover, form a "tent" using heavy-duty foil to cover skewers while grilling.

Italian Sausage Kabobs (page 27).

Use a plastic bag for marinating. Twist and seal top. Turn occasionally to marinate all pieces.

Cut pineapple into wedges. Remove core and cut fruit from rind (do not remove rind).

Chicken Legs Caribbean (page 45).

Turkey and Vegetable Barbecue (page 51).

Rotisserie Polynesian Pork

½ cup pineapple juice
½ cup vegetable oil
½ cup dark corn syrup
¼ cup lime juice
1 small clove garlic, finely chopped
2 tablespoons packed brown
    sugar
1 tablespoon prepared mustard
1 tablespoon soy sauce
2 teaspoons salt
1 teaspoon ground coriander
½ teaspoon ground ginger
4 - pound fresh pork boneless blade
    Boston roast, rolled and tied

Mix all ingredients except pork roast; pour over pork. Cover and refrigerate, turning pork occasionally, at least 8 hours.

Remove pork. Insert spit rod lengthwise through center of pork; hold firmly in place with adjustable holding forks. Cover and cook pork on rotisserie about 4 inches from low heat until done and no longer pink in center (170°), 3 to 3½ hours. Cut into serving pieces.   12 servings.

Peachy Ham on the Rotisserie

½ cup peach preserves
1 tablespoon chili sauce
1 tablespoon lemon juice
⅛ teaspoon ground cloves
⅛ teaspoon liquid smoke
1½ - pound fully cooked boneless
    smoked ham

Mix all ingredients except ham; reserve. Insert spit rod lengthwise through center of ham; hold firmly in place with adjustable holding forks.

Cover and cook ham on rotisserie about 4 inches from low heat until done (140°), 50 to 60 minutes; brush ham 2 or 3 times with reserved peach preserve mixture during last 15 minutes of cooking. Cut into serving pieces. Serve remaining peach preserve mixture with ham. Garnish with peach halves sprinkled with snipped parsley if desired.   6 servings.

Barbecued Ham on the Rotisserie

6 - pound fully cooked boneless
    smoked ham
1 can (8¼ ounces) crushed
    pineapple
1 cup packed brown sugar
2 tablespoons lemon juice
1 tablespoon prepared mustard

Score fat on ham in diamond pattern. Insert spit rod lengthwise through center of ham; hold firmly in place with adjustable holding forks. Mix remaining ingredients.

Cover and cook ham on rotisserie about 4 inches from low heat until done (140°), 2½ to 3 hours; brush ham 2 or 3 times with pineapple mixture during last 15 minutes of cooking. Cut into serving pieces.   20 servings.

Curried Lamb Patties

1 pound ground lamb (or mixed
    with 15% lean ground beef)
1 teaspoon curry powder
½ teaspoon ground coriander
½ teaspoon onion powder
½ teaspoon lemon pepper
4 slices bacon

Mix all ingredients except bacon. Shape mixture into 4 patties, each about 4 inches in diameter. Wrap bacon slices around edge of each patty and secure with wooden picks.

Grill patties about 4 inches from medium coals, turning once, until done and no longer pink, 5 to 7 minutes on each side for medium.   4 servings.

Lamb Shish Kabobs

2 teaspoons salt
¼ teaspoon coarsely ground
    pepper
½ to 1 teaspoon ground oregano
2 pounds lamb boneless shoulder,
    cut into 1½-inch cubes
1 small onion, thinly sliced
2 medium green peppers, cut into
    1½-inch pieces
1 pound large fresh mushroom
    caps

Mix salt, pepper and oregano; sprinkle over lamb cubes and onion slices. Cover and refrigerate at least 2 hours.

Discard onion slices; thread lamb cubes on each of 6 metal skewers. Alternate green pepper pieces and mushroom caps on each of 4 metal skewers, leaving space between foods.

Cover and grill lamb kabobs 5 to 6 inches from medium coals, turning 4 or 5 times, until lamb is done, 30 to 35 minutes. Cover and grill vegetable kabobs 5 to 6 inches from medium coals until green pepper is crisp-tender, 15 minutes. 6 servings.

Lamb and Vegetable Kabobs

½ cup vegetable oil
⅓ cup lemon juice
1 clove garlic, finely chopped
2 teaspoons salt
1 teaspoon dried dill weed
¼ teaspoon coarsely ground
    pepper
1½ pounds lamb boneless
    shoulder, cut into 1¼-inch
    cubes
4 small whole tomatoes
2 large ears corn, cut into 2-inch
    pieces

Mix oil, lemon juice, garlic, salt, dill weed and pepper; pour over lamb cubes. Cover and refrigerate, turning lamb 2 or 3 times, at least 4 hours.

Remove lamb; reserve marinade. Thread lamb cubes and vegetables separately on metal skewers, leaving space between foods. Insert 2 skewers parallel and about ½ inch apart through center of tomatoes to keep tomatoes from slipping when they are turned.

Cover and grill lamb kabobs 5 to 6 inches from medium coals, turning once, until done, about 20 minutes. Cover and grill vegetable kabobs, brushing 2 or 3 times with reserved marinade, 15 minutes.   4 servings.

Grilled Lamb Chops

Cover and grill 2 pounds lamb shoulder chops, about ½ inch thick, 5 to 6 inches from medium coals, turning and brushing 2 or 3 times with one of the sauces (below), until lamb is of desired doneness, 12 to 18 minutes for medium. Serve with any remaining sauce.   6 servings.

Orange Ginger Sauce

¼ cup frozen orange juice
        concentrate, thawed
¼ cup soy sauce
1 teaspoon crushed fresh
        gingerroot

Mix all ingredients.

Mint Garlic Sauce

½ cup mint-flavored apple jelly
2 tablespoons water
2 cloves garlic, crushed

Heat all ingredients over medium heat, stirring constantly, until jelly is melted.

Red Currant Sauce

½ cup red currant jelly
1 tablespoon prepared mustard
1 tablespoon soy sauce

Heat all ingredients over medium heat, stirring constantly, until jelly is melted.

Red Wine Herb Sauce

¼ cup dry red wine
¼ cup chili sauce
¼ teaspoon dried oregano leaves,
        crushed
¼ teaspoon dried thyme leaves,
        crushed
¼ teaspoon dried rosemary leaves,
        crushed

Mix all ingredients.

Leg of Lamb Barbecue

4- to 5-pound leg of lamb, boned
2 small cloves garlic, peeled and
    slivered
½ cup red wine vinegar
⅓ cup vegetable oil
⅓ cup packed brown sugar
2 tablespoons dried tarragon
    leaves
1 teaspoon salt
2 green onions (with tops), cut
    into 2-inch slices
1 can (8 ounces) tomato sauce

Trim excess fat from lamb; if necessary, cut lamb to lie flat. Cut 4 or 5 slits in lamb with tip of sharp knife; insert garlic slivers in slits. Mix remaining ingredients except tomato sauce; pour over lamb. Cover and refrigerate, turning lamb 2 or 3 times, at least 8 hours.

Remove lamb; stir tomato sauce into marinade. Cover and grill lamb 5 to 6 inches from medium coals until done (175°), 50 to 60 minutes; turn lamb every 10 minutes and brush 2 or 3 times with marinade mixture during last 10 minutes of grilling. Remove garlic slivers; cut lamb into serving pieces.   14 servings.

Minted Leg of Lamb

½ cup packed brown sugar
½ cup vegetable oil
1 teaspoon grated lemon peel
¼ cup lemon juice
3 tablespoons vinegar
¼ cup snipped fresh mint leaves
1 teaspoon dried tarragon leaves
1 teaspoon salt
1 teaspoon dry mustard
4- to 5-pound leg of lamb, boned,
    rolled and tied
    Fresh mint leaves

Mix all ingredients except leg of lamb and whole mint leaves. Heat to boiling; reduce heat. Simmer uncovered 5 minutes; cool. Pour over lamb. Cover and refrigerate, turning lamb 2 or 3 times, at least 24 hours.

Remove lamb. Arrange hot coals around edge of firebox; place water-filled foil drip pan under grilling area. Add whole mint leaves to hot coals. Cover and grill lamb over drip pan and 5 to 6 inches from medium coals until done (175°), 2½ to 3 hours. Add fresh mint leaves and coals every 30 minutes to maintain smoke and even heat. Cut lamb into serving pieces.   14 servings.

Polynesian Veal Cutlets

1 can (8¼ ounces) crushed
    pineapple, drained (reserve
    syrup)
½ cup coarsely chopped water
    chestnuts
6 veal cutlets (about 1½ pounds),
    about ¼ inch thick
6 slices bacon
½ cup catsup
2 tablespoons soy sauce
1 clove garlic, crushed

Mix pineapple and water chestnuts. Spread 2 tablespoons pineapple mixture on half of each veal cutlet; fold into halves. Wrap 1 slice bacon around each cutlet; tie securely with heavy string. Mix remaining ingredients and reserved pineapple syrup.

Cover and grill veal 5 to 6 inches from medium coals, turning once and brushing 4 or 5 times with catsup mixture, until veal is tender, 25 to 35 minutes.   6 servings.

Microwave Reheat Directions: For 1 serving, place refrigerated veal on microwaveproof plate. Cover loosely and microwave on medium (50%) until hot, 1½ to 2½ minutes. Let stand 2 minutes. For 2 servings, microwave 3 to 4 minutes.

POULTRY
for the Barbecue

Simple Grilled Chicken

1   teaspoon salt
¼   teaspoon pepper
3 - pound broiler-fryer chicken,
        cut up
¼   cup margarine or butter, melted

Mix salt and pepper; rub on chicken pieces. Cover and grill chicken, bone sides down, 5 to 6 inches from medium coals 15 to 30 minutes; turn chicken. Cover and grill, turning and brushing 2 or 3 times with margarine, until chicken is done, 20 to 40 minutes longer.   6 servings.

Minted Chicken and Fruit

¼   cup snipped fresh mint leaves
2   tablespoons margarine or
        butter, softened
2   tablespoons honey
2   teaspoons prepared mustard
2½ - pound broiler-fryer chicken,
        cut up
1   can (16 ounces) peach halves,
        drained
1   can (16 ounces) pear halves,
        drained

Mix mint leaves, margarine, honey and mustard. Cover and grill chicken pieces, bone sides down, 5 to 6 inches from medium coals 15 to 30 minutes; turn chicken. Cover and grill, turning 2 or 3 times, until chicken is almost done, 10 to 30 minutes; brush chicken with mint mixture.

Place peach and pear halves in well-greased hinged wire grill basket. Cover and grill, turning basket and brushing fruit with mint mixture 2 or 3 times, until chicken is done and fruit is warm, about 10 minutes. Serve fruit with chicken.   6 servings.

Lemon Chicken

½ cup dry white wine
¼ cup lemon juice
2 tablespoons vegetable oil
1 teaspoon paprika
1 lemon, thinly sliced
1 clove garlic, crushed
3 - pound broiler-fryer chicken, cut up
1 lemon, thinly sliced
  Paprika

Mix wine, lemon juice, oil, 1 teaspoon paprika, 1 lemon and the garlic; pour over chicken pieces. Cover and refrigerate at least 3 hours.

Remove chicken and lemon slices. Discard lemon slices; reserve marinade. Cover and grill chicken, bone sides down, 5 to 6 inches from medium coals 15 to 20 minutes; turn chicken. Cover and grill, turning and brushing 2 or 3 times with reserved marinade, until chicken is done, 20 to 40 minutes longer. Roll edges of lemon slices in paprika; arrange around chicken. 6 servings.

Quick-Dip Lemon Chicken

¼ cup frozen lemonade concentrate, thawed
2 tablespoons grenadine syrup
1 tablespoon vegetable oil
1 teaspoon onion salt
2½ - pound broiler-fryer chicken, cut up

Mix all ingredients except chicken pieces. Dip chicken in mixture. Cover and grill chicken, bone sides down, 5 to 6 inches from medium coals 15 to 30 minutes; turn chicken. Cover and grill, turning and brushing 2 or 3 times with lemonade mixture, until chicken is done, 20 to 40 minutes longer.   6 servings.

Wine-Marinated Chicken

¾ cup dry red wine
¼ cup lemon juice
1 tablespoon instant minced onion
½ teaspoon salt
½ teaspoon aromatic bitters
2½ - pound broiler-fryer chicken, cut up

Mix all ingredients except chicken pieces; pour over chicken. Cover and refrigerate at least 1 hour.

Remove chicken; reserve marinade. Cover and grill chicken, bone sides down, 5 to 6 inches from medium coals 15 to 20 minutes; turn chicken. Cover and grill, turning and brushing 2 or 3 times with reserved marinade, until chicken is done, 20 to 40 minutes longer.   6 servings.

REHEATING CHICKEN IN THE MICROWAVE

If you have leftover grilled chicken, cool quickly, cover and refrigerate, no longer than 3 or 4 days. To reheat, place 1 serving of refrigerated chicken on microwave-proof plate. Cover loosely and microwave on high (100%) until hot, 1 to 1½ minutes. Let stand 1 minute. For 2 servings, arrange pieces with thickest parts to edge of plate; microwave 2 to 3 minutes.

Honey-Glazed Chicken

½ cup honey
2 tablespoons vegetable oil
2 tablespoons prepared mustard
2 tablespoons lemon juice
½ teaspoon grated lemon peel
½ teaspoon salt
2½-pound broiler-fryer chicken,
　　cut up

Mix all ingredients except chicken pieces. Cover and grill chicken, bone sides down, 5 to 6 inches from medium coals 15 to 30 minutes; turn chicken. Cover and grill, turning and brushing 2 or 3 times with honey mixture, until chicken is done, 20 to 40 minutes longer.　6 servings.

Chicken Afghanistan

¾ cup plain yogurt
2 tablespoons lemon juice
1 tablespoon vegetable oil
1 teaspoon salt
1 clove garlic, crushed
1 teaspoon ground cumin
1 teaspoon ground ginger
1 teaspoon paprika
1 teaspoon almond extract
2½-pound broiler-fryer chicken,
　　cut up
1 lemon, thinly sliced
　Paprika

Mix yogurt, lemon juice, oil, salt, garlic, cumin, ginger, 1 teaspoon paprika and the extract; pour over chicken pieces. Cover and refrigerate at least 1 hour.

Remove chicken; reserve marinade. Cover and grill chicken, bone sides down, 5 to 6 inches from medium coals 15 to 30 minutes; turn chicken. Cover and grill, turning and brushing 2 or 3 times with reserved marinade, until chicken is done, 20 to 40 minutes longer. Sprinkle lemon slices with paprika; arrange on chicken.　6 servings.

Chicken Legs Caribbean

¼ cup dark rum
1 tablespoon chili powder
1 tablespoon molasses
¼ teaspoon red pepper sauce
4 chicken drumsticks
4 chicken thighs
　Grilled Pineapple (right)

Mix all ingredients except chicken pieces and Grilled Pineapple; pour over chicken. Cover and refrigerate at least 1 hour.

Remove chicken; reserve marinade. Cover and grill chicken, bone sides down, 5 to 6 inches from medium coals 15 to 20 minutes; turn chicken. Cover and grill, turning and brushing 2 or 3 times with reserved marinade, until chicken is done, 20 to 40 minutes longer. Serve with Grilled Pineapple.　6 servings.

Grilled Pineapple

Cut off top of medium-size ripe pineapple. Cut pineapple lengthwise into 6 wedges; cut off pineapple core. Loosen fruit by slicing from rind (do not remove rind). Drizzle ¼ cup honey over fruit; let stand 1 hour.

Grill pineapple, rind side down, 5 to 6 inches from medium coals until heated through, 20 to 25 minutes.

Chicken Wings Oriental

1/4 cup chili sauce
1/4 cup soy sauce
1/4 cup vinegar
2 tablespoons honey
1 tablespoon vegetable oil
2 teaspoons chili powder
1/2 teaspoon garlic powder
18 chicken wings (3 to 4 pounds)

Mix all ingredients except chicken wings; pour over chicken. Cover and refrigerate at least 1 hour.

Remove chicken; reserve marinade. Cover and grill chicken 5 to 6 inches from medium coals, turning and brushing 2 or 3 times with reserved marinade, until chicken is done, 20 to 35 minutes.   6 servings.

Island Chicken

1/2 cup chili sauce
1/4 cup finely chopped onion
2 tablespoons vegetable oil
2 tablespoons vinegar
1 tablespoon steak sauce
1 teaspoon garlic salt
1/2 teaspoon dry mustard
1/4 teaspoon pepper
2 1/2 - pound broiler-fryer chicken, cut into quarters

Mix all ingredients except chicken quarters. Cover and grill chicken, bone sides down, 5 to 6 inches from medium coals 20 to 35 minutes; turn and brush chicken with chili sauce mixture. Cover and grill, turning and brushing 2 or 3 times with chili sauce mixture, until chicken is done, 25 to 45 minutes longer. Cut into serving pieces.   6 servings.

Fiery Chicken

3/4 cup tomato and yellow chili
      sauce with onions
1 to 2 teaspoons chopped hot or
      mild green chilies
1 tablespoon chili powder
1 tablespoon vegetable oil
2 1/2 - pound broiler-fryer chicken, cut
      into quarters

Mix all ingredients except chicken quarters. Cover and grill chicken, bone sides down, 5 to 6 inches from medium coals 20 to 35 minutes; turn and brush chicken with chili sauce mixture. Cover and grill, turning and brushing 2 or 3 times with chili sauce mixture, until chicken is done, 25 to 45 minutes longer. Cut into serving pieces.   6 servings.

COVERING UP

Covered cooking ensures even doneness. If your grill doesn't have a cover, improvise a cover or "tent" by loosely tucking heavy-duty foil over the food and the grill. Cover chicken pieces, and you'll get moist insides with a golden brown, soft skin. Grilled uncovered, your chicken will be drier inside with a darker brown, crispier skin.

Cranberry-Glazed Chicken

1/4 cup dry red wine
1 teaspoon cornstarch
1/2 cup jellied cranberry sauce
1 tablespoon margarine or butter
1/4 teaspoon salt
1/4 teaspoon ground cinnamon
2 1/2 - pound broiler-fryer chicken, cut
   into quarters

Mix wine and cornstarch. Mix in remaining ingredients except chicken quarters. Cook over medium heat, stirring constantly, until mixture thickens and boils; remove from heat.

Cover and grill chicken, bone sides down, 5 to 6 inches from medium coals 20 to 35 minutes; turn and brush chicken with cranberry mixture. Cover and grill, turning and brushing 2 or 3 times with cranberry mixture, until chicken is done, 25 to 45 minutes longer. Cut into serving pieces. Serve with jellied cranberry sauce if desired.   6 servings.

Curried Chicken Barbecue

3/4 cup plain yogurt
1/4 cup lemon juice
1 tablespoon curry powder
1 teaspoon ground ginger
1 teaspoon salt
1/2 teaspoon ground cinnamon
1 clove garlic, crushed
2 1/2 - pound broiler-fryer chicken, cut
   into quarters

Mix all ingredients except chicken quarters; pour over chicken. Cover and refrigerate at least 1 hour.

Remove chicken; reserve marinade. Cover and grill chicken, bone sides down, 5 to 6 inches from medium coals 20 to 35 minutes; turn chicken. Cover and grill, turning and brushing 2 or 3 times with reserved marinade, until chicken is done, 25 to 45 minutes longer. Cut into serving pieces.   6 servings.

Chicken Breasts Italian

1/2 cup dry red wine
2 tablespoons olive or vegetable
   oil
2 teaspoons Italian herb
   seasoning
2 cloves garlic, crushed
3 whole chicken breasts (about
   2 pounds), cut into halves

Mix all ingredients except chicken breasts; pour over chicken. Cover and refrigerate at least 1 hour.

Remove chicken; reserve marinade. Cover and grill chicken, bone sides down, 5 to 6 inches from medium coals 10 to 20 minutes; turn chicken. Cover and grill, turning and brushing 2 or 3 times with reserved marinade, until chicken is done, 25 to 35 minutes longer. Cut into serving pieces. Garnish with ripe olives, cherry tomatoes and parsley if desired.   6 servings

Chicken Breasts Paprika

1/4 cup margarine or butter,
    softened
1 tablespoon paprika
1 teaspoon salt
1/4 teaspoon pepper
2 cloves garlic, crushed
3 whole chicken breasts (about 2
    pounds), cut into halves

Mix all ingredients except chicken breasts. Cover and grill chicken, bone sides down, 5 to 6 inches from medium coals 10 to 20 minutes; turn chicken. Cover and grill, turning and brushing 2 or 3 times with margarine mixture, until chicken is done, 25 to 35 minutes longer. 6 servings.

Chicken Breasts Teriyaki

1/4 cup soy sauce
1/4 cup sweet white wine
1 tablespoon sugar
1 tablespoon vegetable oil
1 teaspoon crushed gingerroot or
    1/4 teaspoon ground ginger
1 clove garlic, crushed
2 whole chicken breasts (about
    1 1/2 pounds), boned, skinned
    and cut into halves

Mix all ingredients except chicken breasts; pour over chicken. Cover and refrigerate at least 1 hour.

Remove chicken; reserve marinade. Cover and grill chicken 5 to 6 inches from medium coals 10 to 20 minutes; turn chicken. Cover and grill, turning and brushing 2 or 3 times with reserved marinade, until chicken is done, 10 to 20 minutes longer. 4 servings.

Rotisserie Cornish Hens

3 frozen Rock Cornish hens
    (about 1 1/4 pounds each),
    thawed
1 teaspoon salt
1 can (6 ounces) frozen orange
    juice concentrate, thawed
1/4 cup catsup
2 tablespoons soy sauce
1/2 teaspoon dried tarragon leaves

Rub cavities of hens with salt. Flatten hen wings over breasts; tie with heavy string to hold securely. Tie legs together, then tie to tails. Insert spit rod through cavities of hens from breast ends toward tails; hold firmly in place with adjustable holding forks. Mix remaining ingredients.

Cover and cook hens on rotisserie about 4 inches from low heat until done (leg bones move easily), 1 1/4 to 2 hours; brush hens 2 or 3 times with orange juice mixture during last 10 minutes of cooking. Heat remaining orange juice mixture until warm. Cut hens lengthwise into halves. Serve with orange juice mixture. 6 servings.

Wine-Basted Hens

3 frozen Rock Cornish hens
   (about 1¼ pounds each),
   thawed
1 teaspoon salt
¼ cup red currant jelly
¼ cup dry red wine
1 tablespoon margarine or butter
½ teaspoon garlic powder

Cut hens lengthwise into halves; rub cut sides with salt. Heat remaining ingredients over medium heat, stirring constantly, until jelly is melted.

Cover and grill hens, bone sides down, 5 to 6 inches from medium coals, 20 to 35 minutes; turn hens. Cover and grill, turning and brushing 2 or 3 times with jelly mixture, until hens are done, 25 to 35 minutes longer. Serve with any remaining jelly mixture.   6 servings.

Herb-Smoked Chicken

3 cups hickory wood chips
3-pound broiler-fryer chicken
½ teaspoon ground sage
½ teaspoon ground oregano
1 tablespoon each dried tarragon
   leaves, oregano leaves and
   parsley flakes

Cover hickory chips with water. Let stand 30 minutes; drain.

Rub outside and cavity of chicken with sage and ground oregano. Flatten chicken wings over breast; tie with heavy string to hold securely. Tie legs together, then tie to tail. Insert barbecue meat thermometer so tip is in thickest part of inside thigh muscle and does not touch bone.

Add 1 cup hickory chips to hot charcoal. Fill water pan with water. Add tarragon, oregano and parsley to water pan. Place chicken, breast side up, on rack about 6 inches from water pan over coals. Cover smoker and smoke-cook chicken, adding charcoal and soaked hickory chips every hour, until done (185°), 4 to 6 hours (add water to pan during cooking if necessary). Cut into serving pieces.   6 servings.

Note: Smoked poultry is pinker in color than roasted poultry.

Spicy Rotisserie Chicken

¼ cup lemon juice
2 tablespoons vegetable oil
1 teaspoon chili powder
½ teaspoon paprika
½ teaspoon salt
1 clove garlic, crushed
3-pound broiler-fryer chicken

Mix all ingredients except chicken. Flatten chicken wings over breast; tie with heavy string to hold securely. Tie legs together, then tie to tail. Insert spit rod through cavity of chicken from breast end toward tail; hold firmly in place with adjustable holding forks.

Cover and cook chicken on rotisserie about 4 inches from low heat until done (leg bone moves easily), 1½ to 2 hours; brush chicken 2 or 3 times with lemon juice mixture during last 15 minutes of cooking. Cut into serving pieces.   6 servings.

Garlic Chicken on the Rotisserie

2 tablespoons lemon juice
2 tablespoons vegetable oil
1 teaspoon dried oregano leaves
½ teaspoon garlic powder
5 cloves garlic, crushed
½ teaspoon salt
2½-pound broiler-fryer chicken

Mix lemon juice, oil, oregano and garlic powder; reserve. Mix garlic and salt; rub cavity of chicken with salt mixture. Flatten chicken wings over breast; tie with heavy string to hold securely. Tie legs together, then tie to tail. Insert spit rod through cavity of chicken from breast end toward tail; hold firmly in place with adjustable holding forks.

Cover and cook chicken on rotisserie about 4 inches from low heat until done (leg bone moves easily), 1½ to 2 hours; brush chicken 2 or 3 times with reserved lemon juice mixture during last 15 minutes of cooking. Cut into serving pieces.   6 servings.

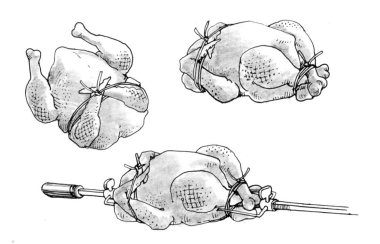

Grilled Turkey Legs

4 turkey drumsticks
1 tablespoon salt
¼ cup soy sauce
2 tablespoons vegetable oil
1 tablespoon lemon juice
2 teaspoons crushed fresh
   gingerroot or 1 teaspoon
   ground ginger
1 teaspoon dry mustard
2 cloves garlic, crushed

Place turkey drumsticks and salt in Dutch oven; add enough water to cover. Heat to boiling; reduce heat. Cover and simmer until tender, 1 to 1½ hours; drain.

Mix remaining ingredients; pour over turkey. Cover and grill turkey 5 to 6 inches from medium coals, turning and brushing 4 to 6 times with marinade, until turkey is done, 40 to 60 minutes. Cut turkey from bone to serve.   8 to 10 servings.

Grilled Turkey Burgers

1 package (16 ounces) ground
   turkey
¼ cup dry bread crumbs
2 teaspoons instant minced onion
1 teaspoon prepared horseradish
½ teaspoon ground sage

Mix all ingredients. Shape mixture into 4 patties, each about 4 inches in diameter. Grill patties about 4 inches from medium coals, turning once, until desired doneness, 5 to 7 minutes on each side for medium. Serve in hamburger buns with cranberry relish if desired.   4 servings.

Turkey and Vegetable Barbecue

8- to 10-pound turkey
2 teaspoons salt
¼ teaspoon cayenne pepper
2 onions, cut into fourths
   Vegetable oil
   Thyme Butter (right)
   Roasted Potatoes (right)
   Roasted Corn (right)
   Grilled Tomatoes (right)

Rub cavity of turkey with salt and cayenne pepper; place onions in cavity. Fold wings across back with tips touching. Tie legs together with heavy string, then tie to tail. Brush turkey with oil. Insert barbecue meat thermometer so tip is in thickest part of inside thigh muscle and does not touch bone.

Arrange hot coals around edge of fire box; place foil drip pan under grilling area. Cover and grill turkey, breast side up, 5 to 6 inches from drip pan, brushing occasionally with Thyme Butter, until breast meat is white when pierced with knife (185°), 3 to 4 hours. Add potatoes, corn and tomatoes as directed below. Add coals during cooking to maintain even heat. Let turkey stand 15 minutes before carving. Serve with Roasted Potatoes, Roasted Corn and Grilled Tomatoes.   10 to 12 servings.

Thyme Butter
Mix 2 tablespoons margarine or butter, softened, and ½ teaspoon ground thyme.

Roasted Potatoes
Rub baking potatoes with margarine or butter, softened. Place on cooking grill. Cover and grill, turning once, until tender, 1 to 1½ hours.

Roasted Corn
Husk ears of corn and remove silk. Rub corn with margarine or butter, softened. Place on cooking grill. Cover and grill until tender, 25 to 35 minutes.

Grilled Tomatoes
Cut thin slice from stem ends of tomatoes. Sprinkle tomatoes with grated Parmesan cheese; dot with margarine or butter. Place tomatoes on cooking grill. Cover and grill until heated through, 10 to 15 minutes.

Rotisserie Luau Turkey

¼ cup pineapple juice
2 tablespoons soy sauce
2 tablespoons honey
½ teaspoon ground ginger
8- to 10-pound turkey

Mix all ingredients except turkey. Flatten turkey wings over breast; tie with heavy string to hold securely. Tie legs together, then tie to tail. Insert spit rod through cavity from breast end toward tail; hold firmly in place with adjustable holding forks.

Arrange hot coals around edge of fire box; place foil drip pan under grilling area. Cover and cook turkey on rotisserie about 4 inches from low heat until breast meat is white when pierced with knife (185°), 3½ to 4 hours; brush turkey 2 or 3 times with pineapple juice mixture during last 30 minutes of cooking. Add coals during cooking to maintain even heat. Let turkey stand 15 minutes before carving. Garnish with sliced pineapple and mandarin orange segments if desired.   10 to 12 servings.

Smoked Turkey

3 cups hickory wood chips
8- to 10-pound turkey
2 teaspoons poultry seasoning
1 onion, cut up
1 carrot, cut up
1 celery stalk, cut up

Cover hickory chips with water. Let stand 30 minutes; drain.

Rub outside and cavity of turkey with poultry seasoning. Place vegetables in cavity of turkey. Flatten turkey wings over breast; tie with heavy string to hold securely. Tie legs together, then tie to tail. Insert barbecue meat thermometer so tip is in thickest part of inside thigh muscle and does not touch bone.

Add 1 cup hickory chips to hot charcoal. Fill water pan with water. Place turkey, breast side up, on rack about 6 inches from water pan over coals. Cover smoker and smoke-cook turkey, adding charcoal and soaked hickory chips every hour, until done (185°), 7 to 8 hours (add water to pan during cooking if necessary). Let turkey stand 15 minutes before carving.   10 to 12 servings.

ADDING FLAVOR

If you would like to add a smoky taste to your food, but don't have a smoker, don't despair. Soak hickory, green hardwood or fruitwood chips in water for 30 minutes, drain and toss onto the hot coals and you've got smoke. You can add a different flavor and aroma by sprinkling the hot coals with soaked and drained dried herbs. Try fresh herbs and garlic cloves, too.

FISH and SEAFOOD
for the Barbecue

Cod Kabobs Maui

½ cup dry white wine
1 tablespoon vegetable oil
1 teaspoon dried rosemary leaves
½ teaspoon salt
1 bay leaf, crushed
1 pound cod fillets, cut into 1-inch
  pieces
1 jar (16 ounces) whole onions,
  drained
1 can (8¼ ounces) pineapple
  chunks, drained
6 apricots, cut into halves

Mix wine, oil, rosemary, salt and bay leaf; pour over fish pieces. Cover and refrigerate at least 1 hour.

Remove fish; reserve marinade. Alternate fish pieces, onions, pineapple chunks and apricot halves on each of 6 metal skewers, leaving space between foods. Cover and grill kabobs 5 to 6 inches from medium coals, turning and brushing 2 or 3 times with reserved marinade, until fish flakes easily with fork, 10 to 15 minutes. Serve with hot cooked rice if desired.   6 servings.

Teriyaki Fillets

1½ pounds cod, haddock or
   halibut fillets, about 1 inch
   thick
¼ cup lemon juice
2 tablespoons soy sauce
1 tablespoon vegetable oil
2 cloves garlic, crushed

If fish fillets are large, cut into 8 serving pieces. Mix all ingredients except fish; pour over fish. Cover and refrigerate at least 1 hour.

Remove fish; reserve marinade. Cover and grill fish about 4 inches from medium coals, turning once and brushing occasionally with reserved marinade, until fish flakes easily with fork, 12 to 20 minutes. Garnish with lemon wedges and parsley sprigs if desired.   8 servings.

Oriental Fish Fillets

2 tablespoons frozen orange juice
    concentrate, thawed
1 tablespoon soy sauce
1 tablespoon honey
1 tablespoon vegetable oil
½ teaspoon onion powder
1 pound cod, haddock or halibut
    fillets, ½ to ¾ inch thick

Mix all ingredients except fish fillets; pour over fish. Cover and refrigerate at least 1 hour.

Remove fish; reserve marinade. Cover and grill fish about 4 inches from medium coals, turning once and brushing 2 or 3 times with reserved marinade, until fish flakes easily with fork, 12 to 20 minutes. Cut into serving pieces. Garnish with orange slices and parsley sprigs if desired.   6 servings.

Dilled Cod

¼ cup lemon juice
1 tablespoon vegetable oil
½ teaspoon dried dill weed
½ teaspoon onion powder
½ teaspoon paprika
½ teaspoon salt
⅛ teaspoon red pepper sauce
1 package (11½ ounces) frozen
    cod portions, thawed

Mix all ingredients except fish portions; pour over fish. Let stand uncovered 15 minutes.

Remove fish; reserve marinade. Cover and grill fish about 4 inches from medium coals, turning once and brushing occasionally with reserved marinade, until fish flakes easily with fork, 12 to 20 minutes. Garnish with fresh dill weed and lemon wedges if desired.   4 servings.

Freezer-to-Grill Fish

2 tablespoons lemon juice
2 tablespoons vegetable oil
1 tablespoon snipped chives
1 tablespoon snipped parsley
½ teaspoon dried tarragon leaves
1 package (16 ounces) frozen fish
    fillets
2 medium tomatoes, cut into 6
    slices
¼ cup shredded Cheddar cheese

Mix lemon juice, oil, chives, parsley and tarragon; brush on frozen block of fish. Reserve remaining mixture.

Cover and grill block of fish about 4 inches from hot coals, turning once and brushing occasionally with reserved lemon juice mixture, until fish flakes easily with fork, 20 to 30 minutes. Cut into serving pieces. Top each serving with tomato slice and about 2 teaspoons cheese. Serve on toasted English muffins if desired.   6 servings.

Smoked Salmon (page 61).

Mediterranean Snapper (page 57) and Au Gratin Potatoes (page 66).

Smoky Mackerel Fillets

2 tablespoons lemon juice
1 tablespoon vegetable oil
1 teaspoon Worcestershire sauce
1 teaspoon sugar
1 teaspoon salt
½ teaspoon liquid smoke
1 pound mackerel fillets
  Paprika

Mix all ingredients except fish fillets and paprika; pour over fish. Cover and refrigerate at least 1 hour.

Remove fish; reserve marinade. Cover and grill fish on lightly greased grill about 4 inches from medium coals, turning once and brushing occasionally with reserved marinade, until fish flakes easily with fork, 8 to 12 minutes. Sprinkle with paprika. Cut into serving pieces. Garnish with pimiento-stuffed olives and parsley sprigs if desired.   6 servings.

Confetti Fish in Foil

2 slices bacon, cut into ½-inch
    pieces
3 green onions (with tops), cut
    into ¾-inch pieces
1 green pepper, cut into ¾-inch
    pieces
1 stalk celery, cut into ¾-inch
    pieces
1 medium tomato, cut into
    ¾-inch pieces
½ teaspoon salt
⅛ teaspoon pepper
1 package (14 ounces) frozen pike
    fillets, thawed
1 tablespoon plus 1 teaspoon
    lemon juice

Cook and stir bacon, onions, green pepper and celery until vegetables are crisp-tender, 3 to 5 minutes. Stir in tomato, salt and pepper; remove from heat. Divide fish fillets among four 12-inch squares of heavy-duty aluminum foil. Sprinkle each fillet with 1 teaspoon lemon juice; top each with about ½ cup bacon-vegetable mixture. Wrap securely in foil.

Grill packets about 4 inches from hot coals, turning once, until fish flakes easily with fork, 20 to 30 minutes.   4 servings.

Mediterranean Snapper

½ cup spaghetti sauce
2 tablespoons lime juice
1 teaspoon dried oregano leaves
½ teaspoon salt
1 or 2 cloves garlic, crushed
1½ pounds red snapper fillets, ½ to
    ¾ inch thick

Mix all ingredients except fish fillets; pour over fish. Cover and refrigerate at least 1 hour.

Remove fish; reserve marinade. Cover and grill fish about 4 inches from medium coals, turning once and brushing 2 or 3 times with reserved marinade, until fish flakes easily with fork, 15 to 25 minutes. Cut into serving pieces. Garnish with lime wedges and watercress if desired.   6 servings.

Red Snapper Fillets with Flavored Butters

Cut 1½ pounds red snapper or cod fillets, ½ to ¾ inch thick, into 6 serving pieces. Cover and grill fish about 4 inches from medium coals, turning and brushing occasionally with one of the flavored butters (below), until fish flakes easily with fork, 15 to 25 minutes. Cut into serving pieces.   6 servings.

Lemon Butter

- 2 tablespoons butter or margarine, melted
- 1 tablespoon lemon juice
- ½ teaspoon grated lemon peel
- ½ teaspoon Worcestershire sauce

Mix all ingredients.

Mustard Butter

- 2 tablespoons butter or margarine, softened
- 1½ teaspoons dry mustard
- ½ teaspoon lemon pepper

Mix all ingredients.

Parmesan Butter

- 2 tablespoons butter or margarine, softened
- 2 tablespoons grated Parmesan cheese
- ½ teaspoon dried basil leaves
- ½ teaspoon dried parsley flakes

Mix all ingredients.

Garlic Butter

- 2 tablespoons butter or margarine, softened
- ½ teaspoon paprika
- ½ teaspoon dried oregano leaves
- 1 clove garlic, crushed
  Dash of freshly ground pepper

Mix all ingredients.

Five-Spice Snapper

¼ cup tomato juice
2 tablespoons lemon juice
2 tablespoons soy sauce
1 tablespoon vegetable oil
2 teaspoons five-spice powder
1 pound red snapper fillets

Mix all ingredients except fish fillets; pour over fish. Cover and refrigerate at least 1 hour.

Remove fish; reserve marinade. Cover and grill fish about 4 inches from medium coals, turning once and brushing occasionally with reserved marinade, until fish flakes easily with fork, 15 to 25 minutes. Cut into serving pieces. Garnish with cherry tomatoes and ripe olives if desired.   4 servings.

Pineapple-Ginger Fish

1 can (8¼ ounces) crushed
    pineapple
¼ cup chopped green onions
    (with tops)
2 tablespoons lime juice
1 tablespoon vegetable oil
1 tablespoon honey
1 teaspoon ginger
1 teaspoon salt
1½ pounds halibut, salmon or
    swordfish steaks, ¾ to 1 inch
    thick

Heat pineapple (with liquid), onions, lime juice, oil, honey, ginger and salt to boiling over medium heat, stirring occasionally. Reduce heat; simmer uncovered 3 minutes. Remove from heat.

Cover and grill fish about 4 inches from medium coals, turning once and brushing occasionally with pineapple mixture, until fish flakes easily with fork, 10 to 15 minutes. Cut into serving pieces. Serve with any remaining pineapple mixture. Garnish with sliced pineapple and green onions if desired.   6 servings.

Lemon Fish Steaks

¼ cup lemon juice
3 tablespoons snipped chives
2 tablespoons vegetable oil
1 teaspoon dried dill weed
1 teaspoon paprika
½ teaspoon salt
1½ pounds halibut, salmon or
    swordfish steaks, ¾ to 1 inch
    thick

Mix all ingredients except fish steaks; pour over fish. Cover and refrigerate at least 1 hour.

Remove fish; reserve marinade. Cover and grill fish about 4 inches from medium coals, turning once and brushing 2 or 3 times with reserved marinade, until fish flakes easily with fork, 10 to 15 minutes. Cut into serving pieces. Garnish with thin cucumber slices if desired.   6 servings.

Monterey Fish Steaks

1½ pounds swordfish, halibut or
     salmon steaks, ¾ to 1 inch
     thick
1 teaspoon salt
¼ teaspoon pepper
¼ cup margarine or butter,
     melted
1 tablespoon lemon juice
1 teaspoon dried chervil leaves
     Avocado Sauce or Caper
       Sauce (right)
     Lemon wedges

Sprinkle fish steaks with salt and pepper. Mix margarine, lemon juice and chervil. Cover and grill fish about 4 inches from medium coals, turning once and brushing 2 or 3 times with margarine mixture, until fish flakes easily with fork, 15 to 25 minutes. Cut into serving pieces. Serve with Avocado Sauce or Caper Sauce and lemon wedges. 6 servings.

Avocado Sauce

1 small avocado, cut up
⅓ cup dairy sour cream
1 teaspoon lemon juice
¼ teaspoon salt
     Few drops red pepper sauce

Beat all ingredients with hand beater until smooth.

Caper Sauce

1 lemon
¼ cup capers
1 tablespoon margarine or butter
1 tablespoon snipped parsley
¼ teaspoon salt

Pare and chop lemon, removing seeds and membrane; mix with remaining ingredients. Heat until hot.

Crab-Stuffed Rainbow Trout

6 rainbow trout (8 ounces each
     dressed weight)
     Salt
1 can (7¾ ounces) crabmeat,
     drained and cartilage
     removed
½ cup finely chopped water
     chestnuts
¼ cup dry bread crumbs
¼ cup mayonnaise or salad
     dressing
½ teaspoon crushed tarragon
     leaves
¼ cup margarine or butter, melted
1 tablespoon lemon juice

Sprinkle cavities of fish lightly with salt. Mix crabmeat, water chestnuts, bread crumbs, mayonnaise and tarragon; toss. Spoon into fish cavities; secure with skewers if necessary.

Mix margarine and lemon juice; reserve. Place fish in well-greased hinged wire grill basket. Cover and grill about 4 inches from medium coals, turning basket once and brushing fish frequently with reserved lemon juice mixture, until fish flakes easily with fork, 16 to 20 minutes. Cut into serving pieces. 12 servings.

Fish with Stuffing

3 cups cooked rice
½ cup mayonnaise or salad
    dressing
½ cup finely chopped water
    chestnuts
⅓ cup chopped green onions
    (with tops)
1 jar (2 ounces) chopped
    pimiento, drained
¾ teaspoon salt
¼ teaspoon pepper
3 pounds whitefish or bass
    (1 or 2 whole fish), cleaned
    Margarine or butter, melted

Mix all ingredients except fish and margarine; spoon into fish cavity. Secure with skewers and lace with string.

Place fish in lightly greased hinged wire grill basket. Cover and grill about 4 inches from medium coals, turning basket once and brushing fish 3 or 4 times with margarine, until fish flakes easily with fork, 30 to 40 minutes. Cut into serving pieces. Garnish with lemon wedges if desired.   6 servings.

Note: Extra stuffing can be heated 30 minutes in covered aluminum foil pan on side of grill.

Smoked Salmon

3 cups hickory wood chips
2 tablespoons margarine or
    butter, melted
2 tablespoons lemon juice
2 tablespoons snipped fresh dill
    weed or 1 teaspoon dried dill
    weed
3 - pound salmon, cleaned

Cover hickory chips with water. Let stand 30 minutes; drain.

Mix margarine, lemon juice and dill weed; brush on both sides of salmon. Add 1 cup hickory chips to hot charcoal. Fill water pan with water. Place salmon on rack about 6 inches from water pan over coals. Cover smoker and smoke-cook salmon, brushing once or twice with lemon juice mixture, until salmon flakes easily with fork (180°), 3 to 4 hours. Add charcoal and soaked hickory chips every hour (add water to pan during cooking if necessary). Cut salmon into serving pieces. Garnish with fresh dill weed and lemon slices if desired.   16 servings.

Grilled Butterfly Shrimp

1 pound fresh raw shrimp (18 to
    20 in shells)
½ cup dry white wine
1 tablespoon snipped parsley
1 tablespoon vegetable oil
1 teaspoon dried basil leaves
½ teaspoon salt
1 bay leaf, crushed
½ lemon, thinly sliced

Peel shrimp. Make a shallow cut lengthwise down back of each shrimp; wash out sand vein. Press each shrimp flat into butterfly shape. Mix remaining ingredients; pour over shrimp. Cover and refrigerate at least 1 hour.

Remove shrimp; reserve marinade. Arrange shrimp in lightly greased hinged wire grill basket. Cover and grill about 4 inches from medium coals, turning basket and brushing shrimp 2 or 3 times with reserved marinade, until shrimp is pink, 6 to 10 minutes. Garnish with lemon slices and, if desired, snipped parsley.   6 servings.

Skewered Shrimp

½ cup Italian salad dressing
1 pound fresh raw shrimp (18 to 20 in shells), peeled and deveined
1 can (8¼ ounces) pineapple chunks, drained
12 whole mushrooms
2 green peppers, cut into 1½-inch squares
18 large pitted ripe olives

Pour salad dressing over all ingredients. Cover and refrigerate at least 1 hour.

Alternate shrimp, pineapple chunks, mushrooms, green peppers and olives on each of 6 metal skewers, placing an olive on end of each skewer; reserve salad dressing. Cover and grill kabobs 5 to 6 inches from medium coals, turning and brushing 2 or 3 times with reserved salad dressing, until shrimp is pink and vegetables are crisp-tender, 10 to 15 minutes.   6 servings.

Scallop Kabobs

1 pound fresh or frozen scallops
2 tablespoons snipped parsley
2 tablespoons vegetable oil
2 tablespoons soy sauce
2 tablespoons lemon juice
½ teaspoon salt
Dash of pepper
1 can (4 ounces) whole mushrooms, drained
12 slices bacon
1 can (13¼ ounces) pineapple chunks, drained

Thaw scallops if frozen. Mix parsley, oil, soy sauce, lemon juice, salt and pepper; pour over scallops and mushrooms. Cover and refrigerate, turning scallops and mushrooms once, at least 30 minutes.

Remove scallops and mushrooms; reserve marinade. Partially fry bacon (just until it begins to curl); drain and cut slices into halves. Alternate scallops, mushrooms, bacon and pineapple chunks on each of 6 metal skewers. Cover and grill kabobs about 4 inches from medium coals, turning and brushing 2 or 3 times with reserved marinade, until scallops flake easily with fork, 12 to 20 minutes.   6 servings.

Grilled Lobster Tails

6 medium fresh or frozen lobster tails
½ cup margarine or butter, melted
⅓ cup lemon juice
2 teaspoons Worcestershire sauce
½ teaspoon onion salt
½ cup margarine or butter, melted
Lemon wedges

Thaw lobster tails if frozen; cut away thin undershell (covering meat of lobster tails) with kitchen scissors. To prevent tail from curling, bend each tail backward toward shell; crack. Mix ½ cup margarine, the lemon juice, Worcestershire sauce and onion salt.

Cover and grill lobster tails, shell sides down, about 4 inches from medium coals 10 minutes, brushing 4 to 6 times with margarine mixture; turn lobster tails. Cover and grill until meat is opaque, 5 to 10 minutes longer. Serve with remaining ½ cup margarine and the lemon wedges.   6 servings.

VEGETABLES and BREADS
for the Barbecue

Vegetable Kabobs

1½ pounds zucchini (about 3
    medium), cut into ¾-inch
    slices
2 green peppers, cut into
    1½-inch pieces
18 cherry tomatoes
18 whole mushrooms
½ cup bottled Italian dressing
1 teaspoon garlic salt

Alternate vegetables on each of 6 metal skewers, leaving space between vegetables. Mix dressing and garlic salt; brush on vegetables.

Cover and grill kabobs 5 to 6 inches from medium coals, turning and brushing 2 or 3 times with dressing mixture, until vegetables are crisp-tender, 10 to 15 minutes.   6 servings.

Smoky Vegetable Kabobs: Cover 1 cup hickory chips with water. Let stand 30 minutes; drain. Add hickory chips to hot coals. Continue as directed.

Grilled Corn

Corn in Foil: For each serving, husk fresh corn and remove silk. Spread margarine on corn; place each ear corn on double thickness of heavy-duty aluminum foil. Sprinkle with salt, pepper and 2 tablespoons water. Wrap securely in foil; twist ends of foil. Place corn on medium coals. Cover and cook, turning once, until done, 10 to 15 minutes.

Corn on the Coals: For each serving, remove large outer husks; turn back inner husks and remove silk. Spread margarine on corn. Pull husks back over ears, tying with fine wire. Grill corn 3 inches from medium coals, turning frequently until done, 20 to 30 minutes.

Grilled Eggplant

⅓ cup vegetable oil
2 tablespoons lemon juice
2 cloves garlic, crushed
2 teaspoons dried oregano leaves,
   crushed
1 teaspoon salt
2 medium eggplants (about 2½
   pounds)
1 cup shredded mozzarella cheese
   (about 4 ounces)

Mix all ingredients except eggplants and cheese. Cut eggplants into 1½-inch slices; dip in oil mixture, coating both sides. Cover and grill eggplants 5 to 6 inches from medium coals until tender, 8 to 12 minutes; turn and brush eggplants 2 or 3 times with oil mixture and top with cheese during last 2 minutes of grilling. 8 servings.

Mushrooms Lyonnaise

2 tablespoons instant minced
   onion
¼ cup water
1 pound fresh mushrooms, sliced
2 tablespoons snipped parsley
½ teaspoon salt
¼ teaspoon pepper
¼ cup margarine or butter

Mix onion and water. Place mushrooms on 18-inch square of double thickness heavy-duty aluminum foil. Sprinkle with onion mixture, parsley, salt and pepper; dot with margarine. Wrap securely in foil. Cover and grill packet 5 to 6 inches from medium coals, turning 2 or 3 times, until mushrooms are done, 15 to 20 minutes.   6 servings.

Onions in Foil

For each serving, wash and cut stem end from 1 medium onion. Cut onion into fourths, not cutting completely through. Place onion on 9-inch square of heavy-duty aluminum foil. Sprinkle ½ teaspoon Worcestershire sauce over onion or brush top of onion with liquid smoke. Wrap securely in foil. Cover and cook onion on medium coals, turning 3 or 4 times, until tender (onion will be soft when pierced with fork), 1 to 1½ hours. Remove outer skin of onion to serve.

Onion and Carrot Kabobs

10 medium yellow onions, peeled
 6 large carrots, scraped and cut
      into thirds
¼ cup molasses
 2 tablespoons prepared mustard
 1 tablespoon vinegar

Heat several inches salted water (½ teaspoon salt to 1 cup water) to boiling. Add onions and carrots. Cover and heat to boiling. Cook until crisp-tender, 10 to 15 minutes; drain. Mix molasses, mustard and vinegar. Alternate onions and carrots on each of 4 metal skewers, leaving space between vegetables. Brush vegetables with molasses mixture. Cover and grill kabobs 5 to 6 inches from medium coals, turning and brushing 2 or 3 times with molasses mixture, until tender, 10 to 15 minutes.   6 servings.

Pea Pod Packets

2 packages (6 ounces each) frozen
      Chinese pea pods
1 can (8 ounces) sliced water
      chestnuts, drained
2 tablespoons soy sauce
1 teaspoon sugar
½ teaspoon onion powder

Rinse frozen pea pods under running cold water to separate; drain. Place pea pods on 18-inch square of double thickness heavy-duty aluminum foil. Top with remaining ingredients; toss. Wrap securely in foil. Cover and grill packet 5 to 6 inches from medium coals, turning 2 or 3 times, until pea pods are hot and crisp-tender, 15 to 20 minutes.   6 servings.

Potatoes in Foil

Choose medium sweet potatoes, yams or white baking potatoes. For each serving, scrub 1 potato and rub skin with vegetable oil or margarine or butter. Wrap potato securely in heavy-duty aluminum foil. Cover and cook potato on medium coals, turning 4 or 5 times, until tender (potato will be soft when pierced with fork), 45 to 60 minutes. Or, cover and grill potato 5 to 6 inches from hot coals, turning 4 or 5 times, until tender, 1 to 2 hours. Cut crisscross gashes through foil and into potato; fold foil back. Squeeze potato gently until some potato pops up through opening. Serve with margarine or butter or dairy sour cream if desired.

Au Gratin Potatoes

1 package (20 ounces) frozen
    French-fried potatoes, thawed
1 cup shredded Cheddar cheese
    (about 4 ounces)
½ cup chopped green onions (with
    tops)
¼ cup half-and-half
2 tablespoons margarine or butter
1 teaspoon salt
½ teaspoon paprika

Place potatoes on 18-inch square of double thickness heavy-duty aluminum foil. Top with cheese, green onions and half-and-half; dot with margarine. Sprinkle with salt and paprika; toss. Wrap securely in foil. Cover and grill packet 4 to 5 inches from medium coals, turning 2 or 3 times, until potatoes are hot and cheese is melted, 20 to 25 minutes. 6 servings.

Potatoes and Onions in Foil

For each serving, cut 1 baking potato into 1-inch-thick slices; brush with melted margarine or butter and sprinkle with salt. Cut onion into 1-inch-thick slices. Reassemble potato with onion slices between slices of potato. Place on double thickness heavy-duty aluminum foil. Brush top with melted margarine or butter; sprinkle with salt and pepper. Wrap securely in foil. Cover and cook on medium coals, turning potato and onion 4 or 5 times, until tender (potato and onion will be soft when pierced with fork), about 45 minutes.

Zesty Grilled Potatoes

Heat 1 inch salted water (½ teaspoon salt to 1 cup water) to boiling. Add 4 medium potatoes. Heat to boiling; reduce heat. Cover and cook until tender, 20 to 25 minutes; drain. While warm, cut potatoes diagonally into ½-inch slices; pour ½ cup bottled Italian dressing over hot slices. Let stand, turning potatoes once, 1 hour.

Remove potatoes. Arrange potatoes in hinged wire grill basket. Cover and grill 5 to 6 inches from medium coals, turning basket 2 or 3 times, until potatoes are golden brown, 20 to 25 minutes. Sprinkle with salt and pepper. 4 to 6 servings.

Grilled German Potato Salad

5 medium potatoes (about
    1½ pounds)
8 slices bacon, crisply fried and
    crumbled
1 cup finely chopped celery
3 green onions (with tops), finely
    chopped
½ cup mayonnaise or salad
    dressing
¼ cup white vinegar
2 teaspoons sugar
1 teaspoon salt
1 teaspoon dry mustard
¼ teaspoon coarsely ground
    pepper

Heat 1 inch salted water (½ teaspoon salt to 1 cup water) to boiling. Add potatoes. Heat to boiling; reduce heat. Cover and cook until tender, 20 to 30 minutes. Drain and cool. Cut potatoes into cubes. Mix potatoes, bacon, celery and onions. Mix remaining ingredients. Pour over potato mixture; toss. Place mixture on 18 x 13-inch piece of double thickness heavy-duty aluminum foil; wrap securely. Cover and grill packet 5 to 6 inches from medium coals, turning 2 or 3 times, until done, 20 to 30 minutes.   4 to 6 servings.

Cheese-Topped Tomatoes

4 large or 8 medium firm tomatoes
1 teaspoon salt
¼ cup dry bread crumbs
½ cup crumbled blue cheese or
    shredded natural Cheddar
    cheese
2 tablespoons margarine or butter

Cut tomatoes crosswise into halves. Sprinkle cut sides with salt, bread crumbs and cheese; dot with margarine. Cover and grill tomatoes, cut sides up, 5 to 6 inches from medium coals until skins pull away from edges of tomatoes, about 10 minutes. 6 to 8 servings.

Italian-Style Zucchini

¼ cup vegetable oil
2 tablespoons vinegar
1 teaspoon dried oregano leaves
1 teaspoon salt
½ teaspoon garlic powder
2 pounds zucchini (about 6 small)

Mix all ingredients except zucchini. Cut zucchini lengthwise into halves; dip in oil mixture, coating all sides. Arrange zucchini in hinged wire grill basket. Cover and grill 5 to 6 inches from medium coals, turning basket 2 or 3 times and brushing zucchini 2 or 3 times with oil mixture, until tender, 12 to 18 minutes.   6 servings.

Barbecue Bread

Cut 1 loaf (1 pound) French bread diagonally into 1-inch slices, cutting almost to bottom of loaf. Spread one of the spreads (below) between slices of bread. Place half of the slices on 14x18-inch piece of heavy-duty aluminum foil; wrap securely. Repeat with remaining slices. Cover and grill bread 5 to 6 inches from medium coals, turning once, until hot, 8 to 10 minutes. Open foil, grill bread uncovered 5 minutes longer.   10 servings.

Blue Cheese Spread

½ cup margarine or butter,
     softened
¼ cup crumbled blue cheese
2 tablespoons grated Parmesan
     cheese

Mix all ingredients.

Parmesan Cheese Spread

½ cup mayonnaise or salad
     dressing
¼ cup grated Parmesan cheese
1 teaspoon dried oregano leaves

Mix all ingredients.

Garlic Chive Spread

½ cup margarine or butter,
     softened
¼ cup snipped chives
1 or 2 cloves garlic, crushed

Mix all ingredients.

Creamy Peanut Butter Spread

1 package (3 ounces) cream
     cheese, softened
3 tablespoons creamy peanut
     butter
1 tablespoon margarine or butter,
     softened

Mix all ingredients.

Stringy Cheese Loaf

1 loaf (1 pound) French bread
1 package (3 ounces) cream
   cheese, softened
1 cup shredded mozzarella cheese
   (about 4 ounces)
¼ cup chopped green onions (with
   tops)
2 tablespoons margarine or
   butter, softened
½ teaspoon garlic salt

Cut bread diagonally into 1 inch slices, cutting almost to bottom of loaf. Mix remaining ingredients; spread between slices of bread. Place bread on 28x18-inch piece of heavy-duty aluminum foil; wrap securely. Cover and grill bread 5 to 6 inches from medium coals, turning once, until cheese is melted, 8 to 10 minutes. Unwrap foil; grill bread uncovered 5 minutes longer.   8 to 10 servings.

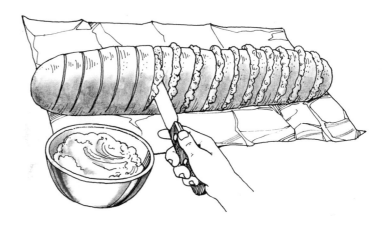

Garlic French Bread

½ cup margarine or butter,
   softened
¼ cup grated Parmesan cheese
2 cloves garlic, crushed
2 tablespoons snipped parsley
1 loaf (1 pound) French bread, cut
   lengthwise into halves

Mix all ingredients except bread; spread on cut surfaces of bread. If necessary, cut bread crosswise into halves. Grill bread, cut sides down, 5 to 6 inches from medium coals until golden brown, 4 to 6 minutes. Cut bread crosswise into 2-inch pieces.   10 servings.

Parmesan Slices

½ cup grated Parmesan cheese
¼ cup margarine or butter,
   softened
   Six 1-inch-thick slices French or
   Vienna bread
1 tablespoon poppy seed

Mix cheese and margarine; spread on both sides of bread slices. Sprinkle with poppy seed. Grill bread 5 to 6 inches from medium coals, turning once, until golden brown, 6 to 8 minutes.   6 servings.

Grilled Texas Toast

1 loaf (1½ pounds) unsliced white
   bread
¾ cup margarine or butter,
   softened
½ teaspoon garlic powder
½ teaspoon seasoned salt

Trim crust from ends of bread; cut bread crosswise into 1½-inch slices. Mix remaining ingredients; spread on both sides of bread slices. Grill bread 5 to 6 inches from medium coals, turning once, until golden brown, 6 to 8 minutes.   10 servings.

Onion-Dill Bagels

6 tablespoons margarine or
   butter, softened
1 tablespoon Dijon-style mustard
1 teaspoon onion powder
½ to 1 teaspoon dried dill weed
6 egg bagels, sliced

Mix all ingredients except bagels; spread on cut surfaces and reassemble bagels. Wrap bagels in individual 9-inch squares of heavy-duty aluminum foil. Cover and grill bagels 5 to 6 inches from medium coals, turning 2 or 3 times, until warm, 8 to 10 minutes.   6 servings.

Seasoned English Muffins

½ cup margarine or butter,
   softened
1 teaspoon chili powder
½ teaspoon onion salt
4 large English muffins, split

Mix margarine, chili powder and onion salt; spread on cut surfaces of muffins. Grill muffins, buttered sides up, 5 to 6 inches from medium coals, turning once, until golden brown, 6 to 8 minutes.   4 servings.

CLEAN-UP TIPS

The one thing all outdoor grills have in common is the cooking grill. And it has to be cleaned — sooner better than later because it's easier. Before cooking, brush the cooking grill with vegetable oil to keep foods from sticking and leaving charred bits. After cooking, whisk (or scrub or scrape) any food particles off with a wire grill brush or a crumpled handful of foil. Wear mitts if the coals are still hot. Small cooking grills can be soaked in hot soapy water.

A gas or electric grill can be cleaned by closing the cover and turning the burner to "high" for several minutes. Turn off the heat and brush cooking grill with a wire grill brush.

Index

NOTES

NOTES